CORVETTE
Richard Nichols

Copyright © 1989 by Brompton Books Corporation

First published in the United States of America in 1989 by The Mallard Press
Mallard Press and its accompanying design and logo are trademarks of BDD Promotional Book Company, Inc.

All rights reserved

ISBN 0-792-45084-1

Printed in Italy

Page 1: Chevrolet dropped the Sting Ray name for 1968, the first year of the new shape bodywork.

Pages 2-3: The last of the old and the first of the new. A 1982 Corvette and a 1984. The difference is obvious, but so is the family likeness.

Below: The return of the Corvette Convertible. A 1988 with its radically raked windshield, rubber band tires and hideaway soft top.

Contents

Showstopper: America's First Sportscar	6
V8 Corvettes: The Birth of a Legend	20
The Real McCoy: The Horsepower Race	30
Sting Ray: The Best Corvette Ever?	44
Operation Mongoose: Corvette Grand Sport	54
Musclecar: The Big Block Years	64
Under Attack: Surviving the Fuel Crisis	84
King of the Hill: The American Supercar	100
Index	127
Acknowledgments	128

Showstopper: America's First Sportscar

The automobile has, since its beginnings, been something which has inspired human emotions to their very heights and depths. From the earliest days of the red-flag wavers right up to the glamor and bustle of the modern-day Grand Prix circuits both the cars and the people associated with them are swathed in romance.

In the nostalgic afterglow of 20/20 hindsight there is a special aura attached to most things associated with the automobile and especially to those parts of it at the pioneering forefront of development, deeply involved in the quest for more power and performance, higher speeds and the technology needed to make it go where steered and to stop when required. In practically every case the development work has taken place on a racetrack somewhere, the need for advance spurred on by the uniquely human competitive spirit and a will to win.

From such a background came the scrapbook of automobilia, peopled with names whose achievements and actions have given them affectionate and revered places in a legend hallowed by time and cataloged by progress. From a past jam-packed with famous names jostling shoulders with each other a few stand a clear head taller than most. Almost anybody could compile their own list and almost all of them would include the names of Ferrari, Aston Martin, Jaguar, Porsche and Mercedes, along with many more. Perhaps not so many of them would also include the name of Corvette. But in the honors list full of cars which went directly from the racetrack to the record books, Corvette stands out as one of the very few cars whose heritage includes Daytona, Sebring, Bonneville and Le Mans and whose reputation, forged in anger, was built on the street, the place for which it was originally conceived.

Of all those famous names only Corvette stands out as a single identity. The others are manufacturers, not marques, but no-one speaks of the Chevrolet Division of General Motors. The name, uniquely, is Corvette.

What other manufacturer's model can claim for itself the distinction of being regarded as a make in its own right, with its own production facility? Only Corvette has eschewed its Chevrolet parentage and stands beyond the pale of corporate identity. Nowhere on the current models will you find the name of Chevrolet, nor their ubiquitous bow-tie symbol. To GM and to the rest of the world, Corvette has been master of its own destiny for years.

Looking at the full history of this outstanding car it's easy to see why. In design and construction it set so many motor industry firsts that it had to be special right from the very first working drawings. In construction the very first Corvettes were made from the revolutionary new material, Glass Reinforced Plastic (GRP), an innovation which still only a very few motor manufacturers have followed almost 30 years later, although even this was part of a chain of events so coincidental it was almost an accident.

Originally conceived as a car to set the postwar college campuses alight and topple the glamorous European sportscars from their dominant position in the two-seat convertible market, Corvette did just that. Right from the start it had the looks, the style, the image and – if only for a while – the muscle. For devotees of the sportscar the Corvette was always 'The One.'

From the start Corvette was designed to combat the European expertise in this market, but for the greater part of its history it lacked the aplomb and deft handling of its chosen competitors. Frequently hailed as the world's only straight-line sportscar, Corvette suffered from a more than slightly lumbering image which although based to a large extent in fact is not altogether borne out by its racetrack record and which was totally dispelled during the eighties. Corvette took 27 Sports Car Club of America National Championships between 1957 and 1976 and, in full race trim, completely defeated the Cobras of Carroll Hall Shelby at Nassau race week during the time when the Ford-based cars were considered invincible. This once-in-a-lifetime victory over the all-conquering Cobras was never repeated. Not because Shelby beat them next time out, but because GM tried to quash the Corvette Grand Sport project before it got to the racetrack and never again put their corporate muscle into a Corvette racing program, although various unofficial entries on worldwide racetracks seemed to have a great deal of backdoor support from GM. In fact there are also several 'private' Corvette racers, including a French lady driver, who you could ask about factory involvement in racing. All through the period of non-involvement and the absence of Corvette works cars from GM there were a number of privateers whose cars went better than might have been expected and who knew things which surprised a lot of fellow-competitors. Those cars, perhaps, owed more to Detroit than anywhere else.

Despite that, and despite its racing strength and success, it was never on

Previous pages: The 1954 Corvette. Only 3640 cars were built that year in a factory designed to produce 10,000 annually.

Below left: One of the first. Some 200 of the 300 Corvettes built in 1953 are known to have survived into the 1980s.

Right: The 1953 Motorama Dream Car. In January it was a prototype, by December they'd hand-built 300 production models. Note the Corvette script above the grille.

Below: 1953. Any color you like as long as it's Polo White with Sportsman Red trim.

the racetrack that the Corvette legend was founded. In the end it was on the street and the sidewalk it happened, and no wonder. For the most electrifying part of the Corvette image has always been its looks. From the very start, in the ballroom of New York's Waldorf-Astoria back in 1953, right up to the present day the Corvette has won most of its following simply because it *looks* like the ultimate sportscar.

Restrained, refined, even classical design has never been the strong point of the US auto industry and even now it seems that the imported European influence has been unable to wean design teams away from the slabby look which has been the hallmark of the American Dream since the immediate postwar years. The elegance of the thirties was brief and has never been recaptured, a fact which has always been true of sedans but never more evident than in the two-seat market. Certainly during the sixties and seventies if you wanted a sportscar then Europe was the place, preferably Italy, and the visionary styling houses of Turin. While France has never excelled, Germany gave us Mercedes and Porsche, Britain offered Jaguar, MG, Morgan, Lotus, Triumph. Only in the eighties did GM design their sportscar range the right way round, and the new-generation Camaro/Firebird/TransAm models were

SHOWSTOPPER: AMERICA'S FIRST SPORTSCAR 11

Left: Over a third of the Corvettes produced in 1954 were left unsold by the end of the year.

Right: 1954 interior with period jukebox styling. Beige was the other choice for 1954.

Below: Red on white was still the predominant color combination for 1954, but no color tags were fixed in 1954 or 1955, so exact verification of numbers is difficult.

designed as full-blooded performers and then detuned. Previously it was back to front, and saloon cars were rebodied to be sportscars, with the engineering teams being left to do the best they could to redeem the legacy of chassis and suspension design totally inappropriate for sportscar performance.

Such was also the situation with Corvette to begin with, although it did change. But styling was ever its strong point and remains so today. Cruising on a freeway or stopped at lights, Corvette always looked aggressive, clothed scantily in the most refined bodywork available. Just looking at it should be enough to make most novice car designers give up and go home.

GM plans for the re-vamp of Corvette for 1984 offended and worried purists the world over. The reality, however, when the new model was unveiled, wasn't too far from the past and has quickly gained acceptance. Even so it is hard to see what even a motor giant could have done to Corvette to still the restless spirit of a legend which has outlived most of its detractors and competitors, survived the fuel crisis, rationalization, several major body changes and lately the Japanese onslaught. Once before the red pen of accountancy has been raised over the Corvette balance-sheet, and it survived that too. Linked, as it is, to some of the most illustrious names in the history of the motor industry, it's no wonder that Corvette has become what it is to so many people.

And Corvette is a story of people too. Not only the names of the famous, like Harley Earl and Zora Duntov, but the unsung, the backroom boys and most of all the people on the street who recognized greatness the minute they saw it and pushed it to the height of success with their acclaim. All have their place. But above the noise of the crowd rises the rumble of Duntov's V8, pushing through the throng comes the curled-lip snarl of the glassfiber wheelarch, just as it did all those years ago, in 1953.

At the New York Motorama in 1953 people stood in line for more than half an hour just to get a look at a white two-seat sportscar revolving on a turntable in front of a mural of the Manhattan skyline. GM inaugurated the Motorama shows in 1949. Traditionally they opened in the ballroom of the Waldorf-Astoria, stayed in New York for ten days and then went on a nationwide tour of major cities. The idea was to create a forum for innovation in the auto industry, allow design teams to show where they were heading and, after the glitter of fantasy had worn off, persuade the public to get their hands on a little bit of the tinsel by buying a GM car.

There were eight such shows between 1949 and 1961, before the advent of TV advertising more or less killed them off. In 1953, as the first experimental color TV broadcasts were taking place in the USA, GM showed Motorama visitors just what they could do. The exhibits included the Pontiac Parisienne Coupe, the Buick Wildcat Roadster, the Cadillac Le Mans Convertible and the Oldsmobile Cutlass two-seat Coupe. Also a white plastic car

Above left: Red wheels, chromey hubcaps with painted inserts, and the all-important whitewall tires. True 1950s details.

Above: Trunk lid lock was hidden away under the bumper, and exhaust pipes exited through the bodywork.

Above right: Convertible top stows away under this rear deck lid. Open the lid, swing the top out, close the lid and clip the top back over it.

Right: Pennant Blue was one of the 1954 color choices, though this example has lost its chrome sidestripes.

Overleaf: You can't help thinking this picture of the Flint, Michigan, plant was mocked up for the camera. Note the early 1953 domed hubcaps and dirty whitewalls on the leading car.

SHOWSTOPPER: AMERICA'S FIRST SPORTSCAR 13

introduced to the world as the Corvette. These, according to GM, are small, fast, highly maneuverable warships. The public (and the press) loved the car. Nothing since the Le Sabre in 1950 had fired their imagination to such a high degree. The difference this time was that, unlike the Le Sabre, Corvette was practical, purposeful and affordable.

Always in the habit of carrying out opinion research at Motorama shows, GM discovered that a very high percentage of people who had seen the car wanted one as soon as possible. But time-lag in the auto industry is traditionally lengthy; it can take years to design and then tool up for a new model. But a demand the size of that which GM were now faced with required sterner measures, and the very first production Corvette rolled off the line in Flint, Michigan, on 30 June of the same year, a scant five months after the debut of the prototype.

Obviously an achievement on this scale involved great numbers of people, but the impetus behind Corvette originally came from only a few. If any man could be said to have 'fathered' the project then it must be Harley Earl, Vice-President (Design) of General Motors. Earl is something of a legend in the US auto industry in his own right. It was he who, in 1925, established GM Art and Color, later, in 1937, to become GM Styling, the very first styling studio in the industry. He also was behind the highly acclaimed Buick Y-Job in 1938, the Le Sabre in 1950 and also the fabulous Corvette XP300 in 1961.

Earl's interest in the two-seater market was fueled by the enthusiasm of the American college youth, all of whom raved continually about the Jaguar and MG sportscars. It was Earl who wanted to create a competitor which

would deal with them on their own level and yet still not cost more than the standard Chevrolet range, meaning that he was aiming for a price between $1300 and $1800.

In order to achieve this it was clear that as many stock parts as possible – including chassis – would have to be used in the construction of the car, thus restricting the design team considerably. At the same time the car was to have the sort of performance and handling which could be expected from its European competitors. At first just a passing fancy, the idea crystallized quickly, and when Earl saw the admittedly attractive Alembic I he realized that fantasy could easily become fact, and began to take on board some practical assistance.

Already working for GM was Ed Cole, then Chief Engineer at Chevrolet and later to become Divisional General Manager and then President of GM. To him was given the job of providing power for the project out of the stock Chevrolet engine range.

Also incorporated was Maurice Olley, an ex-Rolls-Royce suspension engineer who had already taught the US factories all they knew about Independent Front Suspension. His area of responsibility was obvious enough.

And a novice designer, Bob McLean, who had never designed a whole car alone before, was given the task of providing the basis for the entire project.

Later on, of course, the idea was sold to Thomas Keating, General Manager of Chevrolet, and then to GM President Harlow Curtice. But first McLean had to give them something to work with.

Current practice was to begin at the firewall and work round it, but McLean started at the back axle and worked forwards, a technique which horrified his contemporaries but which still produced a design way ahead of anything existing in America at the time.

By the time he'd finished, the car was 102 inches long, with the two passengers as close to the rear axle as could be. The engine was thus brought back seven inches in the chassis and set a full three inches lower than usual. This new layout for the car was accepted by Earl after he'd asked whether that was the way MG and Jaguar did it. When the answer was affirmative he decided that was the way GM would do it too.

This did not involve a stock chassis, however, and a new item, using boxed sidemembers for strength, together with a solid crossmember, had to be created. This new chassis had a solid rear axle with leaf springs and Olley's Independent coil-over front end, which gave a 53/47 weight distribution front and rear. By the time passengers and a reasonable load in the trunk were added, the weight distribution was almost 50/50, which is the ideal setup all designers were striving for.

Meanwhile Ed Cole had been busy with the engine, striving to produce a

SHOWSTOPPER: AMERICA'S FIRST SPORTSCAR 17

Left: One of three variations shown at the 1954 Motorama. Note the external door locks. Other variations included a sports coupe and a station wagon, but poor sales that year put paid to their chances of reaching production.

Above: In 1956 the deck lid gained a lock you could find easily and a badge that left you in no doubt whatever.

useful power output from the 'stove-bolt' six-cylinder engine which was the stock Chevrolet offering, based on a 1941 truck powerplant. This 235ci straight six produced 115bhp at 3600rpm from a 7.5:1 compression ratio and delivered 204lbs/ft of torque at 2400rpm. For Corvette the compression was lifted to 8:1 and, for the first time, aluminum pistons were employed. Another innovation came with the new cam and lifters, giving the highest lift valves (0.45 inches) yet seen in the industry. Along with this came double valve springs and new timing.

In order to follow the stylists' directive that no lumps or bulges mar the lines of the hood, the stock carburetor and intake manifold were scrapped, and Cole used three side-draft Carter carburetors on a new manifold which used exhaust gases to heat it. The muffler manifold itself was also redesigned, along the lines of the then-current hotrodding favorite, and consisted of a simple pair of three-into-one downpipes with two mufflers.

When all this had been done Cole was looking at an engine which now produced a respectable 150bhp at 4200rpm and 223lbs/ft of torque at 2400, which was no mean achievement. The only disappointment was that, since the stock engine was designed to operate in conjunction with the Powerglide automatic gearshift, the Corvette was also equipped with the same unit. No improved or manual option was offered, a marketing error which became readily apparent after the car went on sale.

GM Styling had also been at work preparing the car for production. Almost no changes were made to the prototype before production commenced, but there was little need. The principal feature of the car's appearance was the wraparound windshield which had been a prominent feature of the 1950 Le Sabre and was now possible thanks to improved technology.

But the prototype had been made from a revolutionary new material – Glass Reinforced Plastic, the technology for which had been thoroughly boosted during the war years. Original plans for Corvette were that it should be metal-bodied, and to this end experiments were continuing with a new lightweight metal, Kirksite, which had an admittedly short lifespan. But the real impetus now was speed, as GM strove to get Corvette into production as quickly as possible.

Plans were soon made to construct 300 production models in GRP and then produce a further 12,000 in 1954 from Kirksite. But the tooling for even this easily-pressed metal could not be ready in time, and GM decided to make the following year's 12,000 units in GRP also.

Although the technology existed for GRP bodies, it was in its infancy. GM had already made several pre-production models in GRP and gained the experience necessary to bolt Corvette's 32 major body panels (the largest, at 10 feet by 2 feet, was the underbody) and 32 minor panels together swiftly. Rather than a production line, GM used the system employed today by Lotus and Volvo, in which small groups of technicians assemble individual cars rather than continually affix part A to part B. Fully assembled, the 64 sections weighed only 340lbs.

Pre-production had shown that GRP wasn't a problem-free material. Although it enabled GM to take the revolutionary step of using a wire mesh embedded in the rear deck as a concealed (and highly successful) radio antenna, it also meant that the first car had no electrical capability whatever. They had overlooked the fact that plastic is non-conductive, and the standard practice of using the body as an earth/return for electrical apparatus was impossible, meaning that Corvette had to use almost a complete double loop if the lights were going to work.

But Job 1 did leave the line on 30 June 1953, an almost impossible schedule being achieved after consistent effort from everyone involved. Last-minute holdups meant that some left with different hubcaps or something; not all of that first 300 (all of which were convertibles) looked exactly alike, and slightly less than 200 of them were actually sold before the end of the year.

Nevertheless they offered a respectable alternative to the European imports and there was little or no domestic competition among the slabby sedans which the US manufacturers (and that included Chevrolet themselves) were offering. Harley Earl's ambition to put the car on the market as close to base prices as possible wasn't realized, however, and the 1953 Corvette was listed at just over $3000 FOB Flint. But it fulfilled most, if not all, of his other criteria. At a time when MG were pushing their MGA as a poor man's alternative to the Jaguar XK120 (based on a chassis/engine combination which was already out of date), the Corvette weighed in at 2900lbs, had a top speed of 108mph and reached 60mph from a standing start in 11 seconds, managing the standing quarter in 17.9/77mph. All of which is not very different from the kind of figures which would make modern-day racers in the Production classes reasonably happy.

All of this in the year that Stalin died, Eisenhower and Churchill attended the Bermuda Conference, the Korean War ended and Laos was invaded by the Viet Minh, Hillary conquered Everest, and Russia and Britain exploded their first atomic weapons. However, hampered by a reasonably high price and its convertible-only, two-speed-Powerglide-only options, Corvette failed to fulfill the marketing ambitions of GM almost right from the start. In December of 1953 production was switched from Flint to St Louis in preparation for the 12,000-unit production run of 1954. Only 3265 were eventually made that year, and only 2780 of them (again all convertibles with the two-speed Powerglide) were actually sold to the breathless American public.

Most of the young were doing their streetracing in the cars of the thirties, shoe-horning flathead V8 motors into the Model A and Model B leftovers rapidly filling the junkyards. Real performance was available from Ford's flathead V8 (basically two straight fours stuck together and needing two water pumps, two sets of hoses and so on) with a little bit of effort.

A Belgian-born Russian gentleman had already perfected the ARDUN hemi-head conversion for this motor and increased its power four times over stock. Chevrolet hadn't made a V8 engine for years, and were still relying on revamped equipment which was, as in the case of the straight six, more than ten years old.

Luckily GM could see the future coming just around the corner, and had the foresight to employ the foreigner responsible for the ARDUN conversion. In May 1953, Zora Arkus Duntov accepted employment in the Chevrolet Research and Development department as a result of correspondence with Ed Cole. His first involvement with Corvette was to make alterations to the suspension of an engineering prototype after he'd driven at the proving grounds; later he won his place in the Corvette legend after his work on the V8 motor.

One such engine was already under development when he arrived, destined to become the 265ci which appeared in the 1955 models and which lifted top speed to 118mph and dropped the 0-60 down to 8.8 seconds.

But 1955 was a fair way off. Production, originally at Flint, had moved to St Louis, although partially complete engines were still built at Flint and shipped on. Assembly at St Louis had to be carefully organized to allow a mass-production giant to construct this low-volume specialist car. Obviously what was needed were larger sales. The college-campus idea had not succeeded, largely because Chevrolet failed to follow it. They saw Corvette as a car to which executives and VIP-types aspired. It was September of 1953 before the automotive press got their hands on a Corvette. When they were finally able to write about it, it was in somewhat glowing terms; but this was hardly the best way of selling a new model. Worse still, it wasn't until late 1954 that Chevrolet began to place adverts for Corvette in the auto press, and they still seemed to be trying hardest to promote an exclusive ('for experts only') image rather than one of popular appeal.

Although they sold a high percentage of the 1954 production they made only 700 Corvettes in 1955, but they began the year with a surplus of more than 1000 units. Even the increased performance of the V8 did little to help, and sales for the year were a mere 1600. Corvette looked as near to cancellation as a car could be, and throughout 1955 Chevrolet were under increasing pressure from the GM accountants to close down the Corvette project entirely and bear the losses as best they could. Luckily this pressure was resisted throughout 1955, but it looked as if 1956 could well see the demise of the car altogether. Several things conspired to change this situation.

Perhaps of all years it was 1955 which saw the advent of youth as the dominant factor in many consumer markets, especially those which existed to provide the transitory 'spring-is-in-the-air' products, of which sportscars are definitely a part. It was also the year that saw the advent into real industry of automation, computers and advanced electronic technology. Things were definitely afoot in the postwar world for the first time, and a period of economic buoyancy was fast approaching.

It was also the year in which the Ford Motor Company launched the Thunderbird; a two-seat convertible first shown in Detroit in late 1954 as a 'personal car.'

SHOWSTOPPER: AMERICA'S FIRST SPORTSCAR 19

Below left: A squadron of 1954s. If you still had this lot in your garage you'd be a lucky guy.

Right: The 1957-62 passenger grab handle. Each year the Corvette lettering on the dash inset differed slightly. This is the 1958 version.

Below: Waiting their turn. Pre-1956 in red, with a twin-headlight, late 1950s' version in the foreground.

V8 Corvettes: The Birth of a Legend

22 V8 CORVETTES: THE BIRTH OF A LEGEND

There is no doubt at all that the advent of the Thunderbird played a major part in the GM decision to continue in production with Corvette. Ford had obviously researched the market and felt that it contained lucrative potential; GM would be foolish to back out of it while they had a head start and an existing product.

In addition Corvette offered, in 1955, a V8 engine which may not have been the ultimate but which certainly put it on a level base with the T-bird. Press testing and manufacturers' figures showed that the Ford 'personal car' hit 60mph in 11 seconds compared to the (optional) V8 Corvette's nine.

More importantly, perhaps, was the general opinion that the Thunderbird was simply a scaled-down ragtop version of Ford's big sedans, while the Corvette was a 'true' purpose-built sportscar.

Nevertheless, the plastic-bodied T-bird, which the public saw for the first time in Detroit in late 1954, was an elegantly good-looking automobile, designed to offer comfort and luxury as well as the freedom of the convertible and a sporty image, and it was clear that Corvette would have to be changed if it was to thwart the usurper.

The V8 motor was a project begun under Ed Cole's predecessor, E H Kelley, and which Cole revamped somewhat, lifting the capacity from 231ci to 265. With a 9.25:1 compression ratio, new combustion chambers and a dual-point distributor, plus a single four-barrel Carter carburetor, the V8 produced 210bhp at 5200rpm.

In conjunction with this came a 3-speed, floorshifted manual transmission completely redesigned for the Corvette with close ratios (although not as close as Duntov would have liked) and an all-new coil-spring clutch far superior to the existing Chevrolet diaphragm unit. Offered as an option in 1955, this powerplant really started to make big numbers in 1956 with the styling changes and the manual transmission. 1955 models hit 60mph in 8.8 seconds, 100 in 25.5 and ran a respectable standing quarter at 16.7/83, with a top speed of 118mph. The next model year saw the manual V8s do 60mph in 7.4 seconds, 100 in 20.8 and quarters in 15.9/88, with a top end of 129mph.

Although the speeds were more than vocal in respect of the improvements attainable from the manual transmission, the change would have done sales a great deal of good in any case, since most sportscar enthusiasts at the time felt that 'real' sportscars did not have automatic transmissions or effeminate extras like power windows (standard on the T-bird but optional on the Corvette). Image was all-important. Quite what they made of the power-operated soft top (based on Harley Earl's rain-sensitive top for the Le Sabre) is not certain.

Without doubt the V8, Chevrolet's first since the war, was a major saving factor for Corvette. Equally, it was clear that styling changes were just as necessary if the Corvette's admittedly weak position in the marketplace was to be maintained, never mind improved.

Work on this had been going on throughout 1955, but it wasn't until 1956 that the new body shape was unveiled, even though Chevrolet management had seen it way back in April of 1955. The production model didn't appear quite as the management had first seen it, but the flexibility of producing a

Previous pages: 1956 Corvettes came with the new V8 engine. The optional hardtop set you back an extra 200 bucks.

Left: 1955 taillight with tiny fins. Only 700 1955 Corvettes were sold.

Below left: A 1955 with six-cylinder Blue Flame engine. V8 versions had an enlarged V in the Chevrolet script.

Right: Introduced in 1955, the 265ci V8 finally gave Corvette the power it needed. That year it meant 195bhp at 5000rpm. The V8s were only $170 more on the price of your car.

Below: 1955 dash was virtually the same as the 1954, and just as beautiful.

car in GRP as opposed to a steel body allowed minor modifications in design even at quite a late stage.

Big changes for 1956, though, included the restyled fenders, with headlights standing aggressively proud rather than recessed, the toothy chromed grille, and the scalloped sides. The car had been heavily influenced by both the Mercedes 300SL and also by the La Salle, from which the scallops, hinting at very traditional sportscar outboard fenders, were a direct imitation. Also available for the first time in 1956 was the optional hardtop, first shown to the public at the 1954 Motorama.

Not only did the car now have an engine which was roughly appropriate to its image, rather than the underpowered straight six, but it had also begun to handle properly too. Duntov's early drives in the Corvette had indicated that there was much which could be done to improve the roadholding and handling, and although his work on the suspension and chassis for 1956 resulted in only minor engineering changes, the effect on the car was so dramatic that Duntov was moved to remark that it now 'goes where it's pointed.' This was enhanced by the improved weight distribution – 52/48 with no passengers or luggage – which in itself relied to a large extent on the fact that the new V8 was some 40lbs lighter than the straight six engine.

So when Chevrolet went to the 56 Motorama they took with them a car of which they were justifiably proud and which was for the first time beginning to realize its full potential. The only problem with that was that nobody else in the world really knew very much about it. What they needed was something – some achievement on a suitably grand scale – which would say all there was to say about the improvements made to the car.

Luckily that didn't prove too difficult. They had, in Duntov, someone who was not only an engineer, but also a reasonably experienced race driver. In 1954, while working at Chevrolet as a development engineer, Duntov had been to Le Mans, where the Porsche factory had entered two versions – one 1100cc and one 1500cc – of their four-camshaft Spyder race car. The 1500 was timed wrong and burnt its pistons, but the 1100, with Duntov at the wheel, won its class.

Strangely enough it was later that year at Dundrod, Belfast, that the Spyder won again, the Tourist Trophy being taken by a pair of American

V8 CORVETTES: THE BIRTH OF A LEGEND

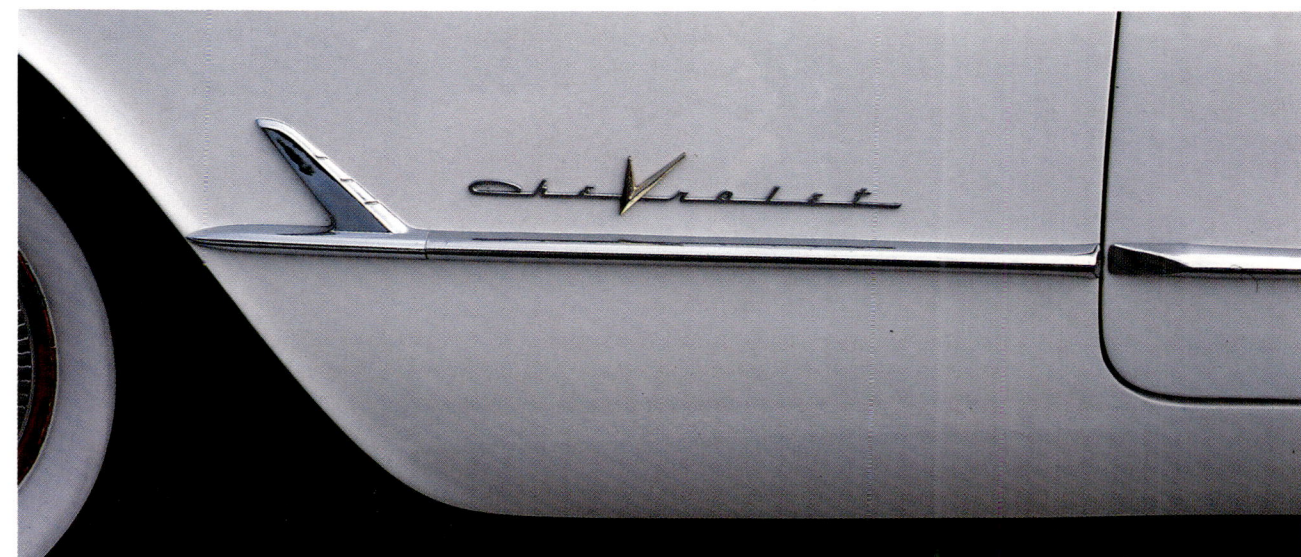

Right: Giant V as part of the Chevrolet side script showed that your 1955 was equipped with the V8 engine.

Below: 1955 in Pennant Red without side trims. Interior trim came in four colors that year, but white was not on the list.

drivers, Masten Gregory and team-mate Carroll Hall Shelby, although that may prove absolutely nothing at all. It was a name which would later crop up in Corvette history, though, and with ominous undertones.

So there was ample justification for allowing Duntov to take off for Daytona Beach in an attempt to put in a record-breaking run before the Motorama debut. He spent a considerable amount of time testing the car on the Chevrolet proving track before he went, and after considerable work, felt that 150mph for the flying mile was a realistic figure.

Aside from bodywork changes to aid airflow slightly, the bulk of his effort went into the engine. His most important modification was eventually the camshaft, which he redesigned to give a lower lift than the stock item but which would take advantage of the engine's characteristics, especially the valve gear. The profile he came up with was unorthodox to say the least but his considerable experience with pushrod racing engines stood him well, and the V8 with a Duntov cam, as it became known, rose from 210bhp at 5200rpm to 240 at 5800rpm. Added to the 10.3:1 high-compression heads used in Modified Sportscar racing the figure went up to 250bhp. So successful was the Duntov cam that it was offered as a factory option on the Corvette and remained an essential item in the building of high-performance Chevrolet V8 engines for years.

Duntov set off for Daytona in late 1955. Weather conditions on the beach were not in his favor, though, and he was unable to make a serious attempt at the record until January of 1956. News of Duntov's record two-way average of 150.583mph reached GM in time for the Motorama.

Now they had something to publicize, even if the car hadn't reached its theoretical maximum of 163mph at 6300rpm or matched the 172mph run recorded by a reputedly stock Jaguar in Europe two years previously. Duntov and his team stayed for the NASCAR (National Associaton for Stock Car Auto Racing Inc) Speed Week in February where, for the first time, Corvette came face to face with the Thunderbird. This was to be a needle match of giant proportions, and more NASCAR rules were bent in those few days than had been in the previous year. Even so, NASCAR (observers of the 150mph run in January) were satisfied that the cars which eventually ran were as legal as they should have been, and that on the timed runs things like the fanbelts weren't prone to 'accidental' slippage at more than 2000rpm.

In the Stock classes the T-bird came out on top, taking first and second, with the Corvette third. Fastest Ford over the standing mile was clocked at 88.77mph, with the Corvette only slightly behind at 86.87, although the Duntov-modified Corvette managed to run 89.75mph. Over the flying mile it was the Corvette which came out as a clear leader – 145.54mph.

All of which was more than convincing, and firmly established the 1956 model as a worthy and supreme successor to the earlier model years. But the show was far from over yet, as no less than four works Corvettes turned up at Sebring after internal pressure at reasonably high level coupled with the general feeling among sportscar racers that the Corvette had great potential. Duntov's work on suspension and steering for 1956 paid off now, as it became clear that the airfield circuit was suited to the car's character, and in a shed on the airfield, work started to prepare the cars for the race.

Engine problems let them down though, when it became clear that it was not possible to set the motors up to run well in both the heat of the day and the cool of the evening. The engineers could manage either time quite

26 V8 CORVETTES: THE BIRTH OF A LEGEND

Left: The 1956 and 1957 models had virtually identical styling. This is the 1956.

Below left: An unusual combination for 1955, Corvette Copper with the white top.

Right: Both 1956 and 1957 had the single headlights and the small fake air intakes on the tops of the front fenders.

Below: 1956 with optional hardtop. The base Corvette was $2900 in 1956. At $185, the signal-seeking AM radio with antenna was nearly as much as a hardtop.

28 V8 CORVETTES: THE BIRTH OF A LEGEND

successfully, but never both. The cars ran poorly, and a 15th overall was the best they could achieve, although they took the over-3500cc class, which wasn't much of a consolation.

GM saw it as a victory, though, and in one respect they were right. Photographs of the dirt-streaked Sebring cars were handed over to the Chevrolet advertising agency and appeared quickly in the press with the copyline 'The real McCoy.' The advert claimed that Chevrolet had produced a car which was at once a well-mannered boulevard cruiser and a fully committed race car. Dubious though this claim may have been, the ad was dramatic enough, and most people saw only the spattered and glamorous image of the race car at work.

The encouragement of Sebring pushed Chevrolet into a full-blooded attempt at the SCCA (Sports Car Club of America) Championship, and the first Corvette raced at Pebble Beach, California, in the hands of Dr Richard Thompson. He drove a hard and winning race, staying in front until the very last moment, when a Mercedes slipped through and relegated him to second overall, although he won his class by a significant margin.

The car went on to race in the Championship as part of a continual development program. After every race Chevrolet engineers would test the car to destruction and then rebuild it in time for the next meeting. But the development program on the racetrack was never anywhere near as significant as the ones taking place off it, although they were both aimed at the same target: to produce visible racing success for the Corvette and thus attain recognition and sales.

Away from the racetrack both Ed Cole and Zora Arkus Duntov were working on a system of fuel injection for the V8 engine in conjunction with John Dolza, a member of the Engineering Division department who had been concerned with fuel injection development for some time already.

The race engine, with high lift cam, bored out to a 283ci displacement, which Duntov had run at Daytona was a clear candidate for fuel injection, and Ed Cole was insistent that it should be available for 1957 models, although this seemed an impossible task. GM had been working at it since the beginning of the fifties, and although it had been successful years before on aircraft, they were unable to adapt it to suit the motor car. Cole was

Right: Venetian Red, Arctic Blue, Cascade Green, Aztec Copper, Onyx Black, Polo White. Beautiful colors for 1957.

Below: 1957 with fuel injection. This option for the 283ci V8 gave it 283bhp, making it one of the more desirable early models.

determined to do it first and in 1957 even though the problems with metering seemed insuperable. Conversation between Dolza and Duntov led to Dolza rethinking his ideas and coming up with a new system of metering. Between them they overcame most of the problems in days, rather than the years which GM had already invested in the project.

The injection system, which was supposed to be fuel-efficient and create less pollution than a normally-carbureted engine, also produced an entirely unexpected bonus. Although on paper and on the rolling road the two kinds of engines checked out as identical, the 283ci with fuel injection produced some ten percent more power than the other. It lifted the 283ci unit from 255bhp right up to 283bhp, producing what everyone accepted as an automotive milestone: one bhp per cubic inch of engine capacity, a fact which Chevrolet were not slow to trumpet to the world. The achievement in this output cannot be denied, no more than can the introduction of the injection system, but it must be remembered that the test engines which were used to arrive at these figures need not have had much relation to those being fitted into the production cars: with longevity of testbed engines not an issue it was quite normal to tune them right up to the absolute limit and quite frequently beyond. Devoid of all engine-driven accessories, without the power-loss associated with transmission and drive-train, it is quite likely that the test engines were producing as much as 50 or 60bhp more than their fully-fitted roadgoing counterparts.

Nevertheless the injection system was proved in anger at Sebring in 1957, when its performance was much aided by a four-speed manual synchromesh transmission which had been produced by GM in conjunction with Borg Warner. This combination gave the Corvette standing quarter miles in the low 14 second bracket with a terminal speed of some 96mph, top speed being quoted at 132mph.

On paper alone this put Corvette in a class of its own. Back in 1953, when the straight six was probably the weakest production engine available in the USA, Corvette had lacked something. With the advent of the smallblock V8 it had gained everything it had lacked and now, in 1957, it had gained something which few people outside the research departments at GM had ever suspected it had lacked, still less could attain.

Dollar-for-dollar comparisons against the T-bird, or even against the Europeans became irrelevant. The Corvette's performance simply made it the fastest car available for the road. Only the hallowed Mercedes 300SL could stand between the Corvette and the record-books, and there was little more than a cigarette paper between them there.

The real tests were to come during the 1957 race season. At Daytona Beach the Corvettes were supreme on both standing and flying mile, taking class honors for both at 91.3 and 131.94mph respectively. And the Corvette experimental model — SR2, rated at around 310bhp — won its class for the standing mile at 93.04, placing second to a D-type Jaguar in the flying mile at 152.86mph.

Daytona, though, was just a warm-up for the main event, the Sebring 12 hours. No more airfield sheds for Chevrolet this time, though, and a full-size hangar was taken over for the works team to operate from. After being second to a Ferrari which retired halfway, Richard Thompson ended twelfth with a convincing class win 20 laps ahead of the nearest Mercedes 300.

Probably more than anything else it was the Sebring win which made Corvette's name and pushed it firmly onto the bottom rung of its 30-year climb to a place in history. No doubt at all either that the injected smallblock was the feature which let it happen. And although it was racing at Sebring in March, the Rochester Ramjet injection system didn't make production until very late in the year: only a few hundred cars were sold with the $400 option, out of a total sale of almost 7000 units.

What shouldn't be overlooked at this point is the major impact made by the new V8 motor. Startling enough in 1955, when it elevated Corvette into the ranks of real sportscars in the finest tradition, by 1957 it was the heart of a true piece of racebred machinery. With the Rochester fuel injection it delivered more horsepower than any other contemporary engine and more than anyone at the time might have expected. Delivering the goods all the way up to 6000rpm at a time when other V8 engines started coming apart at the seams if they reached five, the Chevy smallblock stole the lucrative hotrodding and racing power market back from Ford, whose flathead had dominated it for 20 years. Today the smallblock engine in its various guises is probably the most popular performance engine in the world.

The Real McCoy: The Horsepower Race

Spiritually, if not numerically, it seemed as though the fifties ended in 1958, and the last two years of the decade were a preparation for the years ahead – the swinging sixties.

The first transatlantic commercial jet service had begun in late 1957 and in 1958 London's second airport opened at Gatwick in preparation for the coming boom in world travel. Explorer One, the USA's first Earth satellite, was launched, signaling the very beginning of the Space Age, although it was a while before anybody really noticed.

Chevrolet styling hadn't always been at the forefront of the new wave; they'd probably been the very last to drop the bulbous shapes of the late forties, and their new sedan range didn't make it to the streets until 1955, signaling – in combination with the smallblock V8 – a wave of tremendously elegant cars, getting sleeker each year until the classic 1957 – the same year, you will recall, that Corvette reached what many regard as its peak of excellence.

But elegance was out for 1958. It had been out for most manufacturers the year before, but GM only caught up in 1958. None of their models for that year were as crass as the competiton which had, after all, had a year's start. Big was the order of the day. Most styling houses had begun to chrome plate almost every non-moving part of their cars. The true peak of this, the Cadillac Eldorado, probably the most ostentatious car ever made, didn't feature chrome plate and high tail fins until 1959, but the embryo was all there in 1958.

Ford had recognized this and opted out of what was already an unequal struggle. For 1958 their Thunderbird 'personal car' was a four-seater, offering no opposition to the post of America's only real sportscar which Corvette had earned the previous year.

But the Corvette was not left unsullied by the bad taste which had somehow found its way into auto design studios; for 1958 it grew ten inches in length, two in width and gained 200lbs, taking it for the first time over the 3000lbs curb weight marker. Most of the length hung over the front (wheelbase remained unchanged) and most of the weight came in extra chrome.

Bumpers were enlarged and bolted to the frame, the hood acquired a line of ugly louvers it didn't need and the decklid grew two unpleasant chrome strips which served no purpose whatever. Beside the new grille (nine enormous chrome teeth) there was a pair of chromed dummy scoops – although on serious models a kit to use these to duct cool air to the rear brakes was available – which were also remarkably nasty. The jukebox front end arrived on the Corvette in 1958, and the whole effect was precisely what Styling had wanted – the car looked much bigger than it really was, especially to people lying down in front of it.

Inside, however, Duntov, whose unofficial position as chief of the Corvette production had been made 'legal' in late 1957, was beginning to make his presence felt. At last the tachometer was placed on the steering column where the driver could actually see it, and the dashboard grew a center console pack of instrumentation – the first of its kind and something which has stayed with Corvette right up to the present day.

None of the elaborate chrome gimmickry seemed to affect the car's performance or handling to any real degree, something for which most Corvette owners in 1958 must have been really grateful. There were five engine options available, all variations on the well-proven smallblock, and ranging in power output from a lowly boulevard-cruising 230bhp right through 245, 250 and 270 to the no-holds-barred 290bhp with the Duntov camshaft and fuel injection. In this latter state the Corvette was still a true performance car

Previous pages: As the plate says, a 1960 Corvette. This time in Inca Silver with aftermarket wire spoke wheels.

Left: One of the 1958's chief distinguishing features was the two chrome trunk lid spears.

Below left: Beautiful 1958 in Signet Red. 1958s were thought too flashy at the time so 1959s had less chrome.

Right: 1958 interiors were either red, charcoal, or blue-green. Seats are a hardwearing vinyl which for 1958 had an interesting pebble grain.

Below right: Base 230bhp, 283ci V8 engine. There were four other engine options right up to the 290bhp fuel-injected unit.

and gave the competition, including the thoroughbred Europeans like Jaguar and Ferrari, a highly convincing challenger. However, of the 9000-odd units sold in 1958 only ten percent were the high-performance specification. By far the biggest seller, at 46 percent, was the 230bhp version.

Thankfully 1959 saw more of Duntov's influence at work. To begin with the body styling was much improved to give the sleek grace with which the original Corvette had been conceived. This was attained by the simple expedient of deleting all the unnecessary chromework which had been so offensive on the 1958 model, and restoring the car's rightful elegance. Under the body the suspension had been further improved, with uprated rear springs and a trailing rod system which went some way toward curing the endemic wheelhop which made the back end prance like a racehorse under hard acceleration.

The base-priced model for 1959 was the low output 230bhp version which was sold for $3875 and top of the range was the same 290bhp high performance mode which cost $5127. The extra cash was well spent for those who could afford it. From rest, 60mph came up in only 6.6 seconds, 100mph nine seconds later, and the car would move from standstill to 100mph and stop again in 24.6 seconds, although quarter-mile times stayed much the same as ever at 14.9/98mph. For the most part, and especially with its redesigned seats, the 1959 was well-received. Some press testers felt that it was the best Corvette yet, but that was always qualified with hints about the future.

There was an undercurrent of excitement running through GM at the time, and there were many hints about a better Corvette than ever, as rumors about a brand-new GM sportscar grew and grew. The car, said the rumors, would be entirely revolutionary and create a sensation in the industry when it was announced. For once rumor was true, and it was probably a surprise that the secret had remained a secret for as long as it had. Known as the Q-car, the new sportster was planned with a rear transaxle with transmission and differential in one housing in the back axle, and inboard rear brakes. This technique was planned to improve roadholding enormously, ironing out the very last vestiges of the Eurocars' supremacy over the Corvette when the going got tight and bumpy. Body styling was going to be equally innovative, and the design team were working on a car which would be lower, sleeker,

flatter and sharper than the existing Corvette. It sounds as if they were describing the Stingray, almost the current production models, and that's no coincidence, but it would be four years before anything like the Q-car got on a production line.

In 1958/59 the auto industry was moving slowly into recession, along with the rest of the world. At GM the Q-car (and other similar projects) were stopped and there was a continuing ban on motorsport involvement. It looked as if development of the Corvette, which depended a great deal on information gained on the racetrack, was also suspended. But Harley Earl had been succeeded as Head of Styling by Bill Mitchell and Mitchell's great enthusiasm for racing generally and Corvettes in particular provided much help. Together with Mitchell and Dr Richard Thompson, Duntov began working on a new race car which was eventually to have far-reaching effects.

Meanwhile, the 1960 Corvettes had hit the streets, looking much as had their predecessor. Sales were good, though, possibly thanks to Ford's withdrawal of the Thunderbird, and for the first time topped the 10,000 mark.

Left: The 1958 took the distinctive side side scallop one step further, adding a small scoop with its three chrome spears.

Below left: Lightly customized 1958. Nowadays the trend is toward restoration to the strictest of rules.

Right: 1959 dash, much the same as the 1958 but for the speaker grille surround and the reverse lock-out T-bar on the shifter.

Below right: 1959 also had the smoother hood and no trunk lid spears. The prominent dual headlights lasted right through from 1958 to the total restyle in 1963.

36 THE REAL McCOY: THE HORSEPOWER RACE

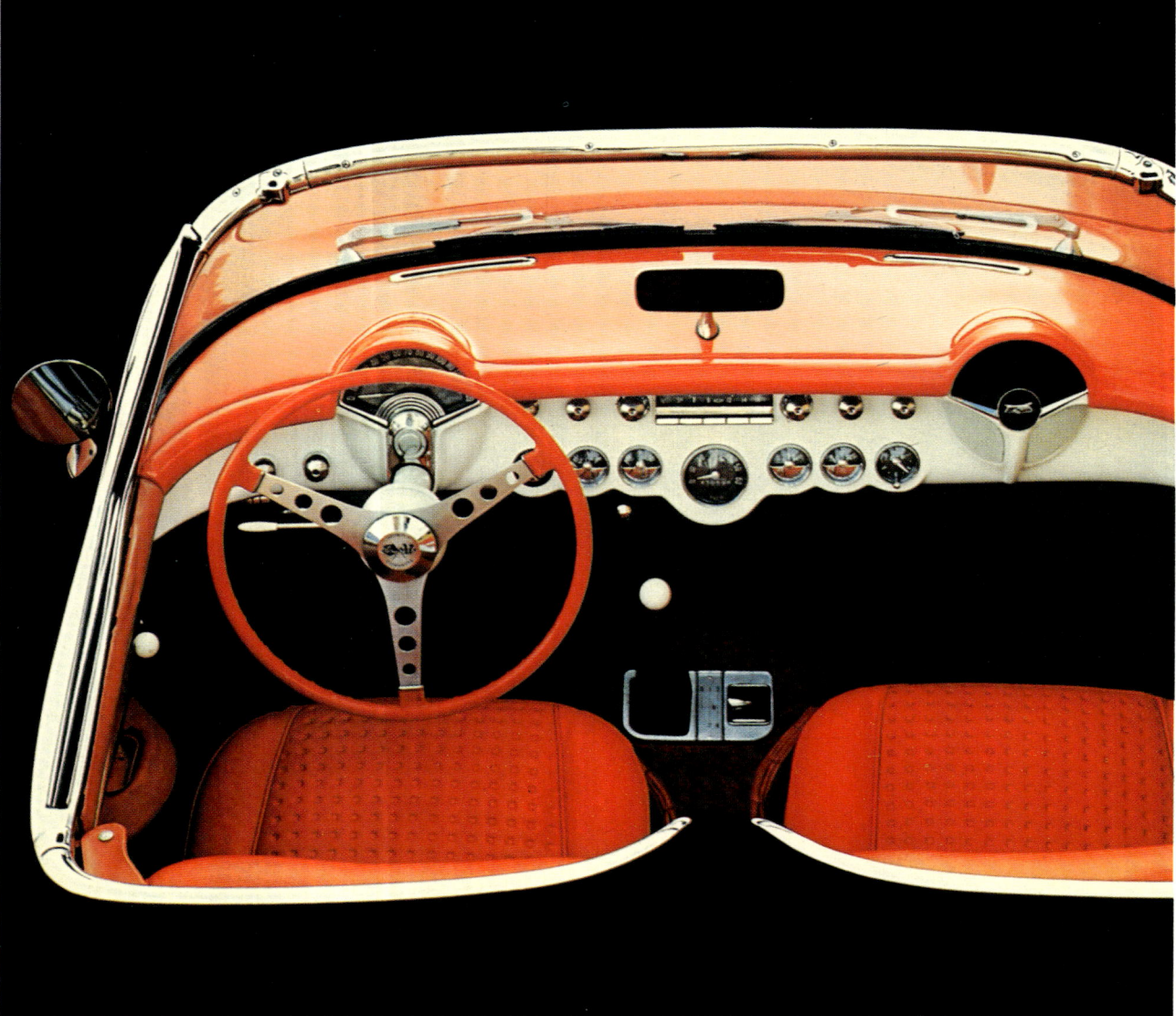

Above left: For 1961, Chevrolet restyled the rear end but left the front more or less unchanged.

Left: Pre-1958 dash had no passenger grab handle, and an array of gauges. Later cars had all the instruments crammed into a cluster behind the steering wheel.

Above right: You don't see many 1960s in Tasco Turquoise, especially with matching turquoise interior. Balance of attractive curves and typical late 1950s chrome epitomizes the early Corvette look.

Right: Nine chrome teeth, two dummy front air vents, bigger bumpers, and dual headlights. The 1958-60 cars took Corvette styling to a peak.

THE REAL McCOY: THE HORSEPOWER RACE 37

THE REAL McCOY: THE HORSEPOWER RACE   39

Left: Corvettes lost their teeth in 1961 and gained a mesh grille instead. Headlight bezels were painted. The 1961 front badge became the twin flags, which for 1962 were circled in a chrome ring.

Above right: The 1961 with its later rearend styling. 1961s retained the chrome trim around and inside the front scallops.

Right and below: The interior changed little from 1958 to 1961. Note the peak in the soft top compartment lid, indicating that this is a 1961. By 1962, the side scallops could no longer be ordered in a contrasting color.

Previous page: 1960 convertible, long, lean and elegant as only Corvette can be.

Left: The venerable 283ci smallblock Chevrolet. 9.5:1 compression ratio, a bore and stroke of 3.875×3 inches, a single four-barrel carburetor and 230hp straight from the factory.

Below: Thick fiberglass bodies and thin chrome trims with fiddly little clips were never the best of combinations, but make all the difference.

Right: The trick with owning an early Corvette is having someone else to clean your chrome. Nine grille teeth, upper and lower grille surrounds, front scoop surrounds, bumpers, and headlight bezels need plenty of elbow grease.

Improvements in the manufacturing setup at St Louis also contributed and trouble-free production became much easier. After the initial breakthrough in 1960, sales continued to rise – almost 11,000 in 1961 and then a rewarding 14,531 in 1962.

The years between 1958 and 1962 were clearly a period of consolidation for the Corvette. It had made its point by 1957, and after the brief chrome-plated aberration of 1958, had settled down as America's only volume-produced sportscar. And although much of the development work – like the Q-car and the XP300 – which had been going on behind the scenes didn't ever make it to the streets, the Corvette was never stagnant.

In 1960 Briggs Cunningham had taken Corvette to Le Mans. In fact there were four competing on the team, the first time the car had appeared on a European racetrack. Although spectators and press alike were enthusiastic about the car's impressive looks, it seemed as if its performance was going to disappoint them, not to mention Cunningham and GM. One car spun off in the rain, one blew an engine, a third completed the 24 hours but had failed to complete the qualifying number of laps and was ruled out as a non-finisher, but the last of them came home in eighth place.

This achievement, coming eighth in the longest and toughest sportscar race in the world, alongside Mercedes, Porsche, Ferrari, Lister-Jaguar and the others, established Corvette as one of the sports road cars of legend on a worldwide basis as well as backing up its unique domestic position.

By 1962 more racetrack lessons had been applied to the Corvette by GM. Hotrodders had for years found the smallblock a highly tuneable and strong engine, and had adopted a practice of enlarging its capacity to 327ci while at the same time porting and polishing the heads.

The 327ci engine, reckoned by many to be the high-point of both small-block engineering and Corvette performance, was offered in 1962 for the first time, and although this didn't have a great deal of effect on its paper performance, and acceleration figures stayed much as they were before, standing quarter-mile times crept along a bit, quoted as near to 14 seconds dead/100mph by various sources as makes no difference.

This absence of apparent improvement owed much to the rear suspension which, despite improvements over the years, still left the back wheels swinging during a hard acceleration more often than they should have been. None of which says anything about the fact that the 327ci engine had definitely made the Corvette a more powerful car to drive on the road. The only visible evidence of this is in the torque figures – the 327 was way way up over the 283, from 295lbs/ft at 5100rpm to 352lbs/ft at 4000rpm.

But despite consolidation and improvements, the Corvette was by now essentially an old car. Although it had progressed beyond recognition from the straight six-powered revolution of 1953 (a car which was by any standards now a slug compared to the current model), it was still in essence a ten-year-old. It was almost a sheep in wolf's clothing, and clearly something had to be done.

Sting Ray:
The Best Corvette Ever?

STING RAY: THE BEST CORVETTE EVER?

It was in 1963 that the revamped Corvette appeared. A revolution in its own right, it can hardly be said to have created the same sort of worldwide fuss as the Beatles who also achieved fame and fortune that year, but it was largely all-new. Work which led eventually to the 1963 model – first shown quietly and politely to the press in October of 1962 – really began way back in the late fifties, because the Stingray was born from the car which was tested at Sebring in 1957, driven briefly by both Juan Manuel Fangio and Stirling Moss and prepared for a works outing at Le Mans which was canceled when the GM ban on race involvement became effective.

The next step was the styling exercise designated as the Q-car, which was also shelved. Bill Mitchell, by now Vice-President of GM, was the man who saved the day, persuading the corporate giant to allow him to continue with the Q-car as an entirely private race-only project. Because of the racing ban, development of this vehicle was funded to a large extent from his own purse, and the new race car bore no Chevrolet identification anywhere on its coachwork. Because of this it was also re-named, and was called the Sting Ray. It was developed in conjunction with its destined driver, Dr Richard Thompson, using basically the same 283ci engine as had powered the 1957 Sebring car, although it now wore 11:1 high-compression aluminum heads.

Its debut was at Marlboro raceway in April of 1959, where its appearance caused an immediate stir. Described by all who saw it as futuristic, the sleek flattened wedge was the center of attention. Futuristic it certainly was, and the element of prophecy in the description applied to it at the time can be seen in production Corvettes right up to the current models, whose lines reflect it to an almost uncanny degree.

Thompson was determined that the car's performance should create as powerful an impression as its looks, and took to the raceway with a will to win only equaled in size by the amount of lead in his right boot. The Sting Ray stayed well in front of the field for most of its debut race, with Thompson driving the kind of race which must have spun his eyeballs in their sockets. Unfortunately they weren't the only thing which spun, and the Sting Ray's brief carousel meant that it finally finished in fourth place overall, which was still an extremely respectable result for a new car straight off the trailer.

The SCCA were not able to agree with this though, and as a result of the Doc's cavalier driving he was suspended from their events for 90 days thanks to body contacts with other race cars in a non-contact formula. Before the car reappeared at an SCCA event it made several runs at USAC events (for which no SCCA license was needed) during which the problem that had caused the spinout on its debut raised its head over and over, indicating quite convincingly that the brakes on the new car were simply not up to racetrack performance.

In June, when the Sting Ray went back into SCCA racing, the problem had still not been sorted. Despite vast 11-inch drums all round the car spun out yet again. The sleek styling didn't help much either. Designed to use the body as an aerofoil, the intended effect was that the flat 'wing' shape should keep the car down, pressed against the tarmac, but in fact the opposite was happening. Shimming the rear suspension to lift the tail and increase the angle of attack through the airflow helped somewhat, but still did nothing to alleviate the braking problem.

The trouble was that the race car's shape allowed it to travel faster than the stock production car. Bodywork on the street cars was clumsy enough, by race standards, to act almost as a dam, and when the driver lifted his foot from the accelerator the drag was enough to start slowing the car down. Deprived of this benefit, and traveling at higher speeds in any case, the race car lost all of the perfectly adequate braking performance which was so much a part of the street car's charm.

In 1960 the Sting Ray went out to race again. This time it had a restyled body, and although the visual changes weren't that important the glassfiber

STING RAY: THE BEST CORVETTE EVER?

Previous pages: All change for 1963. Sleek new purposeful bodystyling heralded the change from boulevard cruiser to serious race-track contender.

Below left: The 1963 coupe's unique split rear window makes it one of the most desirable of Corvettes. If nothing else, it was the first Corvette with a permanent hardtop.

Right: Only the engine and transmission carried over for 1963. The car was called the Sting Ray after Mitchell's one-off race car of the same name. The side exhaust system was only available from 1965-67 and didn't contain a muffler!

Below right: With their sleek sporty looks and ample power, Sting Ray Corvettes were prime customizing targets. This is a 1963 with a 1967 hood. Incredibly, GM didn't fit radials to Corvettes until 1973.

had lost 75lbs in weight over the winter. Larger diameter brake cylinders had improved the stopping power as well, and the handling glitch which had caused most of the old car's problems seemed to have gone for good. The first outing was at Cumberland, and the Sting Ray was better than ever, better than most of the competition. The only thing which stayed in front of it was a thoroughbred Italian race car — a Maserati.

Back at the factory Duntov was still trying to produce the 'revolutionary' new car which had been rumored from Chevrolet for some time. In fact he was trying to find a way to get the Q-car into production in as close to original form as possible. Although this may seem like an easy task, it's not always possible to go ahead and build a car once you know what you want. The biggest single factor in the holdup will always be economics, and this is especially true in the case of cars which have only a low-volume production run. Ideas of genius tend to cost an inordinate amount by the time they reach the showroom, and the whole object of this exercise wasn't only to build cars, but also to sell them.

Attempts to improve Corvette's handling by using a transaxle — carrying the transmission and differential in the same housing on the back axle — while not impractical had produced little effect in weight saving or performance in practical application, especially when compared to cost. In order to give the car the handling qualities he was looking for, it became clear that a mid-engined sportscar was what Duntov wanted.

This was truly revolutionary thinking for a production car in the late fifties. Single-seat race cars, now so familiar with their stressed-member rear-mounted power units, were a long way from the Grand Prix races as yet. Family sedans were still big and slabby. Chevy's own Impala and Biscayne were the cars of 1959 and even the European exoticars were hardly innovative at this period, although they were still hugely expensive. The XKE was pretty, but hardly a revolution in auto design, and Lotus, later to become the sort of excellent and innovative vehicle for which Duntov was presently striving, were hardly past the stage of being a gleam in Colin Chapman's eyes.

But with Ed Cole's assent and backing, Duntov had been looking at the possibility of a mid-engined car in 1958. At the same time, but separately, GM Styling had begun work on a new body for Corvette in 1959, using the now-racing, but privately-entered Sting Ray as a base line for the future production model.

A new chassis was being worked on, to replace the heavy and almost ten-year-old crossmember unit lurking beneath the current production cars. Basis for the new item was to be the lowest possible center of gravity attainable, which left engineers working to a ground clearance of five inches. All major items of mass were to be situated as close to the five-inch line as possible. Working with the existing hardware and a standard front-engine layout, the transmission and engine were set as low and as far back as possible.

A ladder chassis was needed here, and the old crossmember format had to be dispensed with. At the same time the wheelbase was cropped from 102 inches to 98 without making any sacrifices for driver and passenger. But the real advance was at the back. By modifying and using GM production line parts for the front suspension (without detracting from the car) enough money was saved for Duntov to juggle the finances and spend the saving at the back, on independent rear suspension (IRS). This comparatively mild-sounding change altered the weight ratio on the new car drastically. From being biased 51/49 the full IRS car went to 47/53 and for the first time the major part of the weight was at the tail end of the vehicle instead of the front, although the engine stayed where it had always been.

The IRS setup on the 1963 Corvette meant that the solid (and heavy) rear axle could be binned, and with it went a whole third of the unsprung weight and most of the wheel-hop which had dogged the car almost from day one, or at least since the introduction of the smallblock V8 and the arrival of some real power.

Independent rear suspension was not a new idea, and had been used quite widely in race cars. The differential housing is bolted directly to the chassis (which is where most of the weight-saving comes in) and the drive shafts (no longer surrounded by a beam axle and saving even more weight) are used as active members of the rear suspension and dispense with even more metalwork.

Although previously proven on race cars, this arrangement hadn't always worked. In order to allow for the change of angle in relation to the driven rear wheel — which is clearly not a problem with solid rear axles — the outboard end of the driveshaft was splined for several inches, and could then slip backwards out of the hub when necessary. On some occasions though, and especially under load, like heavy acceleration, the splines could lock up and prevent the driveshaft's movement, freezing the rear suspension up solid. It was the careful design work which eliminated this problem that allowed IRS to be fitted to a road-going production car with confidence.

The driveshaft became the upper link in a parallelogram arrangement, with a separate lower link as normal, but instead of the splined arrangement, universal joints at each end of the driveshaft gave it complete freedom of movement while a huge boxy radius arm took care of all the fore and aft movement.

It is puzzling that instead of using coil springs and shock absorbers Duntov left the shock absorbers on their own at each end of the axle and used a transverse leaf spring of the kind most people expected to see on farm tractors and Model T Fords but not on up-to-date sportscars. 'Archaic' was the word most people felt obliged to use in connection with this arrangement, and no wonder.

Nevertheless, it did work, and work very well. In fact the handling was vastly superior to anything Corvette had previously enjoyed, which went a

Above left: 1963 with optional cast aluminum wheels and knock-off hubs; $322 back in 1963, a whole lot more nowadays.

Above: With all the fuss surrounding the 1963 coupe, the Convertible has almost become the poor relation; yet it was still a very stylish car. Note lack of external access to the trunk.

Right: Many 1963 Coupes were converted to the single rear screen in later years, something their owners probably regret nowadays.

STING RAY: THE BEST CORVETTE EVER? 51

Left: Big news for 1965 was disk brakes on all four wheels, which is just as well as some had the new 396ci big-block motor. This is a smallblock Convertible with the slim-line hood bulge.

Above: Sebring Silver brings out the best in this 1963 Coupe's lines.

Right: One-piece rear glass for 1964. The split rear window for 1963 was a controversial innovation and as such was short-lived.

Left: Between 1963 and 1967, the name was Sting Ray. By 1969 it was Stingray.

Right: Interior trim for 1965 came in many colors. This was 'saddle.'

long way to stilling any criticisms of this strangely ancient arrangement. Overall, the new IRS was a superb advance over previous models from the only viewpoint which really counted – behind the wheel. All of which made the cost-saving nine-leaf rear springs worthwhile; it was only economics which caused the car to be built that way, and in fact several pre-production prototypes had been built with coil spring rear suspension but hadn't made it to the street.

Under the skin that left only the brakes to be sorted. Retaining the 11-inch drums, improvement came from increasing their width by ¾ inch at the front and ¼ at the back, raising the total braking surface by almost 30 square inches.

All of this was mounted in the new ladder chassis which weighed almost exactly the same as the old one but which had about 50 percent more torsional stiffness. This may not sound terrifically important, but torsional stiffness is everything to a racer. Shoparound drivers would probably never know the difference since they never drive at the limit, but streetracers and serious competitors would both find out pretty quickly the moment they arrived at a fast corner, and they found the result highly effective and beneficial.

All of this may well be entirely commendable but it was beneath the surface. It was not the new IRS or the larger brake linings which caused small crowds to gather every time a new Sting Ray was parked on a street corner for the first few months of the model life. Nor was it the ladder chassis, the increased space inside created by offsetting the engine to the right and decreasing the size of the transmission tunnel.

Available as a coupe for the first time, it was the completely redesigned body which gained all the attention on the street. Remaining startlingly faithful to the race-only 'private' Sting Ray of Mitchell and Thompson, the Corvette Sting Ray was a new departure in body styling. Not even the European sports models were in the new league. Only the XKE compared in looks in any way and even that looked effeminate compared to the aggressive and positively lupine Sting Ray.

Still identifiably Corvette, the Sting Ray was a dramatic styling advance. The influence of aerodynamics was present in every flattened wedge and every clean line across the bodywork. The sharp-edged point of the hood was retained by pop-up headlights, echoed in the cut-off rear and recessed tail-lights and emphasized in every arrow-straight line across the bodywork.

But the greatest innovation (and the biggest controversy) came with the rear window. The wraparound line was divided straight down the middle by a large piece of fiberglass which spectators and owners either loved or hated. There was no middle line on this one and the feature persisted for only one model year – the 1964 Sting Ray had a one-piece rear window.

For most of 1963 the big customizing trick was to cut the window pillar out and replace the two glass panels with a single piece of plexiglass. When the one-piece glass window came out on the 1964 model even more 1963 cars were butchered in this way; it might have seemed very clever at the time, but most of the people who performed the operation then must be thoroughly repentant now.

The split window was something Mitchell was insistent about, it being very much a left-over from old days with Buick. With questionable wisdom as its basis and the impetus of all the do-it-yourself stylists hacking it out almost straight away, it lasted only that one short year.

It wasn't the only controversial piece of styling on the bodywork, either. The hood louvers, dummies which also only made production for one year back in the fifties and whose demise caused everyone to breathe a sigh of relief, were back for 1963.

This time, though, they had been based on the Q-car, and in that form weren't dummies, serving a working purpose. Around 75 percent of airflow from the radiator core was exhausted through the hood vents, giving the airflow across the car a much easier and smoother ride, while the other 25 percent was used to wash the engine compartment and reduce the buildup of exhaust heat under the hood. On the line, however, they were blanks.

But the Sting Ray represented as much of an advance in the story of Corvette as did the arrival of the injected smallblock all those years previously. Perhaps there was only one thing left to find to create the ultimate musclecar, and as everybody always says, there's no substitute for cubic inches. But the big-block engines were still just around the corner.

Meanwhile there was also trouble around the corner, and it came in the shape of Carroll Shelby. Turned down by GM, Shelby had approached Ford in an attempt to build his own race car and had succeeded. Using an AC chassis and a Ford V8, Shelby was making what was to become the legendary Cobra, a car with similar power to the Corvette but almost a whole 1000lbs lighter.

The 1963 Sting Ray was taken to the racetrack for its debut and won on its very first outing. It was a success which Duntov knew could not be repeated when the Cobra made the raceway, and time soon proved him right. Sting Rays began to suffer a series of humiliating defeats at the hands of the Cobras, and although Duntov didn't believe that this was affecting sales in an appreciable way it was nevertheless hard to come to terms with.

Official Chevrolet opinion, however, was that the SCCA had slipped up with the Cobra, and that it should have been running in C Modified. Although around 900 of them were eventually made only a very few of them, in Chevrolet's estimation, were the full-bore race cars which were inflicting defeat on Corvette. The road-going production Cobra was losing out to road-going Corvettes in the same humiliating way that road-going Corvettes were losing out to Shelby's pure race cars, and the whole thing was a homologation mix-up.

But race reports are the things which get into the public eye, and there was clearly a case for something to be done about the Cobras, and very soon.

Operation Mongoose: Corvette Grand Sport

OPERATION MONGOOSE: CORVETTE GRAND SPORT

The Corvette, it must be realized, is the only production sportscar ever made in America. There have been two-seaters and sports coupes, there have been sporty-looking sedans and four-seat coupes like Camaro and so on which have purported to be sportscars. But in strict definition Corvette is the only one.

Right from its inception in 1953, racetrack development has always played the major part in the development of the car and eventually all of the lessons learned on the track have made their way onto the production line. This is an entirely satisfactory state of affairs and just as it should be. It is also the whole reason that motor manufacturers take their products and their specials to the racetrack in the first place. Detroit-based manufacturers have not been backward at this; in the sixties many factories tried new cars or new engines or simple development work on both racetracks or even on the street. There has always been an amount of illegal streetracing on Woodward, and few factories can deny their occasional night-time presence there with complete honesty.

But in 1957 the big manufacturers agreed that they would not support motor racing any longer. It cost money which at the time they didn't have so much of, and involved them all in tremendous effort to save half a second from a car's lap time simply to beat each other to winning posts which bore no foreseeable relevance to the great bulk of their business, which was turning out sedans for America in ever-larger numbers.

Because of this agreement and the subsequent ban on racing involvement, so much of what Mitchell and Duntov had been doing was far more closely related to the back door of the factory than the front. Had they followed their orders to the letter then the Sting Ray could well have been a stillborn lamb with no teeth instead of the wolf it turned out to be.

But in 1962 Carroll Hall Shelby began to make noises in the direction of GM. His threat was that, in conjunction with Ford, he was about to produce a car which would not only embarrass the 'private' entries which looked a lot like Corvettes and had wild Chevrolet engines, but would blow them completely into the nearest trash can.

No-one at GM knew it at the time, but Shelby was speaking of the legendary aluminum-bodied Cobra. As it turned out he spoke nothing less than the truth, because when the car did appear on racetracks it began to wipe out the opposition without even breathing heavily. Even before the victories at Le Mans the Shelby cars were becoming a legend.

Previous pages: Probably the ultimate development in racing Corvettes, the 1976 Spirit of Le Mans.

Top left: Zora Duntov in the first Corvette V8 prototype at the Milford proving ground.

Center left: Operation Mongoose was the GM name for their attack on the racing Cobras. The full-house racing cars bore the Grand Sport badge.

Below left: Bridgehampton race track in September 1963.

Above right: Sting Ray Corvettes are still being enjoyed on the race tracks.

Right: Duntov is flagged away at the NASCAR Speed Week, Daytona Beach, February 1956.

58 OPERATION MONGOOSE: CORVETTE GRAND SPORT

OPERATION MONGOOSE: CORVETTE GRAND SPORT   59

Left: Silverstone, 3 September 1960. A certain Mr A L Maher takes Becketts in his 'race-weight' Vette.

Below left: Looking more like it had strayed onto the track by mistake, this Corvette makes use of its muscle to stay in contention out of the Esses.

Right: Past the fairground at Le Mans with many hours still to go.

Below: When men were men and racing was racing. Bob Bondurant leads Tony Settember.

60 OPERATION MONGOOSE: CORVETTE GRAND SPORT

Left: In an effort to lose weight for Daytona, this Corvette Grand Sport was cut down to run as a roadster, complete with swoopy roll bar and aerodynamic head restraint.

Right: Grand Sport at Sebring in the summer of 1963.

Below: The NASCAR Speed Week at Daytona Beach back in February 1956. Left to right are Betty Skelton, Zora Duntov, and John Fitch. Corvette had just established its 150mph record.

Corvette owners were getting as much bad feeling from this as GM themselves. No longer king of the street, every corner hid a potential put-down and every bar held a Ford enthusiast who was more than ready to ridicule the first Corvette owner who walked into the room. Even before the Cobras made their debut there were moves afoot to thwart Shelby's attack, and plans were laid to build a Corvette which would without fail be the definitive Cobra-killer. With a touch of pithy wit, plans for Operation Mongoose were laid, and took the form of the Corvette Grand Sport. This was designed to be a homologation special. Under FIA rules 100 cars had to be built as a production item in order to qualify, and by now they were much stiffer about this since Ferrari had managed to get the GTO homologated on a promise and finished up building only slightly more than 30 instead of 100.

The GS looked a great deal like the 1963 Sting Ray, but similarity wasn't even skin deep in this case. For a start the four-layer fiberglass body was drastically thinner and lighter than the stock item although its shape was much the same. The pop-up lights were lost in order to save the weight of the motors which raised them, and four lights were placed on the outboard corners of the nose under a plexiglass fairing. The four-inch filler neck came straight out the side of the body and of course the split window gave way to a one-piece plexiglass wraparound.

The chassis was much the same in layout, except that it used thinner and lighter tubular steel, the differential housing was alloy, the radius arms were drilled through for lightness and the dash was lightweight plastic. Even the seats were buckets on a light tubular frame.

Naturally enough it was the engine which was supposed to be the number one weapon in the war against Shelby. It was to be an all-alloy block, with alloy twin-plug heads along lines already firmly established by Aston Martin. The Rochester fuel injection and the hemispherical combustion chambers gave the 401ci V8 a planned output of around 550bhp and the whole package was designed to bite the Cobra to death on the spot.

Somewhere along the line the GM hierarchy got word of the project and, in a letter to Duntov, President Eric Donner instructed him to abide by the 1957 resolution to refrain from racing involvement. It looked as if the whole project had been killed off without reprieve, but the Cobras were rapidly advancing their own reputations at the expense of Corvette.

By some mysterious process two private race drivers, Dick Doane and Grady Davis, managed to get their hands on a Corvette Grand Sport – one each. Both of them were fast racers and both of them were singularly vague about the origins of their new cars. Quite how they came out of the Chevrolet back door was not something either man was willing to talk about or even acknowledge. Because of the cancellation of Mongoose, neither car had the planned 550bhp alloy block, and both ran the 327ci iron motor. Because the scheduled run of 100 units was no longer viable the cars couldn't run under FIA rules, and wound up competing against pure-bred race cars in SCCA C Modified.

Somewhere along the line a third car appeared from nowhere, along with three of the promised alloy motors. Backdoor help wasn't enough to get them running with fuel injection, and they wound up with Weber carburetors. Thus armed they went to the Nassau Speed Week in December of 1963.

On an overall basis they didn't do that well. Trouble with the differential kept two of them back, trouble with the hood lifting at speed meant that they all had to spend time in the pits and an overall third place for one car was the best posting they could manage over the week. What they did do, though, and do convincingly, was to leave the Cobras behind and put an end to the dominance of the breed and the bad-mouthing Corvette owners were taking at the hands of its supporters.

Still in private hands, and completely unacknowledged by GM, the Grand Sports raced through 1964, two of them cut down to roadsters in an attempt to improve their airflow properties. In the December of 1964 the cars went back to Nassau but this time one had been bought by Roger Penske, who had turned it into a reliable and formidable race car, still with only minimal and illicit help from GM's back door.

Against vast and powerful Cobra opposition Penske sailed to victory with the Corvette and established the last GM victory over the Ford-powered Cobras for years to come. In view of the later successes the Cobra achieved and its later development into the GT40 and the hallowed place in legend enjoyed by this purebred race car it is clearly a shame that GM allowed company politics to sink the Grand Sport without trace, since it obviously could have won for them the reputation enjoyed by the big Fords at Le Mans.

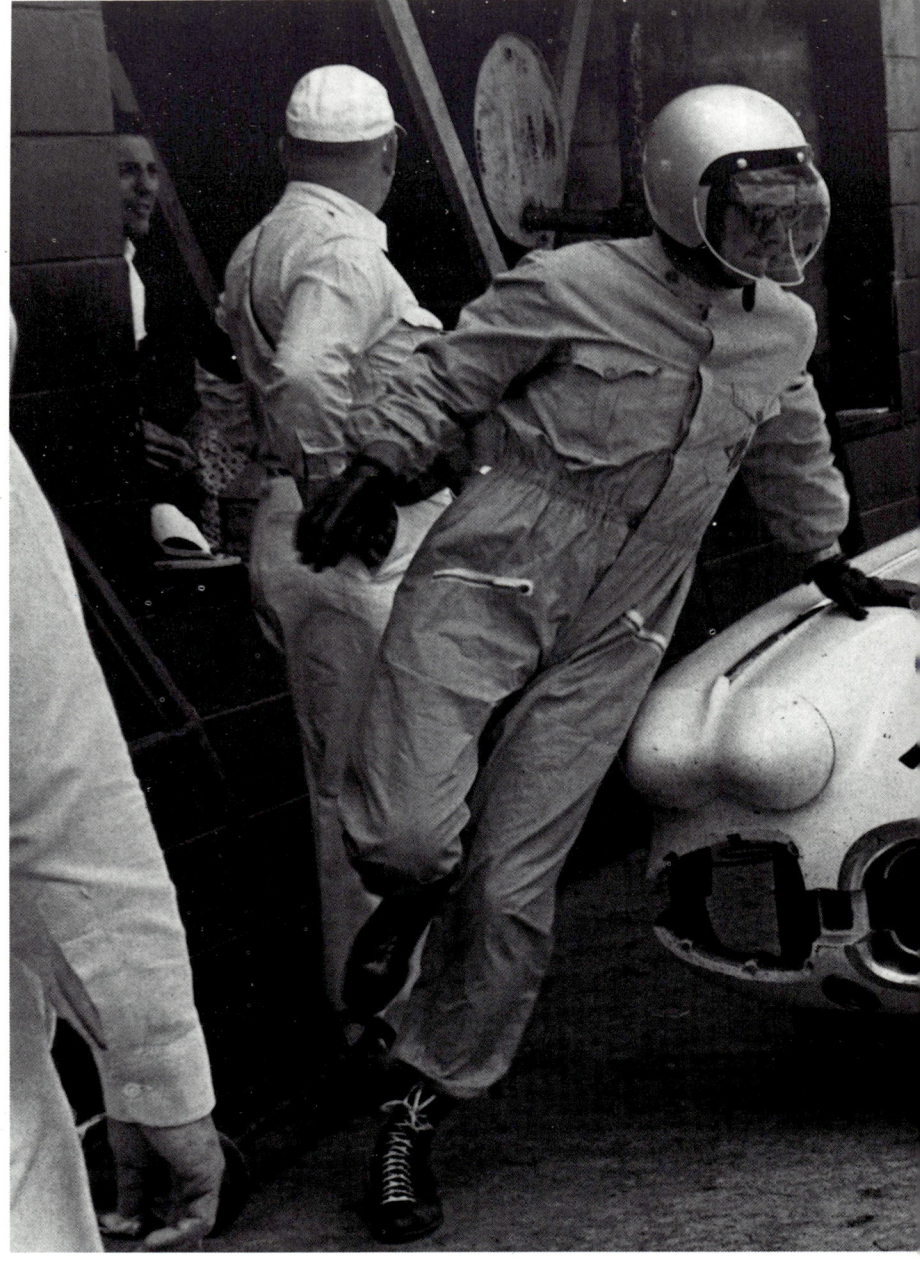

Chevrolet involvement in motor racing, mostly through the Chaparral outfit, has always been more than somewhat covert, and although their successes are undeniable they remain something of a shadow, and Corvette in particular has never been able to claim for itself the place in motor racing history which it deserves and certainly earned.

GM has always been aware of anti-trust legislation and it is possible that dominance on the track as well as over-powering supremacy in the marketplace would have brought them into the public eye to such an extent that such legislative action could well have been the result. But, whatever the reason, it is now only possible for Corvette enthusiasts to mourn the passage into history of a brief interlude which could (and perhaps should) have been much longer.

Much the same story applies to the CERV single-seaters which were a part of the Duntov association with Chevrolet. Designed for the twists of the Pikes Peak hillclimb and the rigors of Indianapolis, the CERV could have been a masterpiece of mid-engined single-seat layout with a hundred new ideas combined on the one car. But like the Grand Sport, CERV was yet another victim of the anti-racing feeling prevalent at GM. Although it appeared briefly at the Peak it didn't run officially. Only present as a moving testbed for Firestone tires, CERV turned in times which appeared slow and only later evidenced themselves as record-breakers. When news of the apparently slow times reached Firestone they backed off and without their support top management at GM wanted no solo role in racing, so the CERV team withdrew from Colorado, leaving their brief and rather ghostly presence as the only mark in the record of Chevrolet involvement.

Once again corporate policy quashed a project of potentially enormous benefit and excitement, and in the light of both these experiences it is sometimes hard to avoid wondering just how the Sting Ray actually made it onto the street at all. Fortunately it did, though, and the 1963 and later models all wore the hallmark of the unofficial race involvement of the Chevrolet staff.

Left: All go at Sebring in 1962. The Johnson/Morgan car with no bumpers.

Below: 30 November 1963. Unloading the Grand Sport Corvettes at Nassau for the Speed Week.

Musclecar:
The Big Block Years

MUSCLECAR: THE BIG BLOCK YEARS

It was in 1964 that the big-inch musclecar machinery began to develop – the Pontiac GTO, more or less epitomizing the unrefined feeling of the moment – and it was in this atmosphere that Chevrolet calmly began to do to the Sting Ray exactly what they'd done to the Corvette in 1959 during the big-finned chrome era, and tone it all down. Indeed, such was the success of the refined 1959 over the gaudy 1958 that it may not be totally out of order to wonder whether or not this was a deliberate policy the second time around.

Body trim was cleaned up all round for 1964 and the most prominent change was the loss of the rear window divider, which at last allowed the driver of the Sting Ray a modicum of rearward vision. Also lost were the dummy hood vents left over on the 1963 from the Q-car.

At the same time as appearance was slightly altered (during a period when major styling changes in the auto industry were mandatory, even if they made a car look worse than it had the previous year) the ride of the Sting Ray was also refined. By use of rubber linkages and stiffer body panels, as well as much improved sound damping, it became quieter and more pleasant to travel in. Gone was the harshness of ride so prevalent in the 1963 – and especially noticed by European testers.

Under the hood hydraulic lifters meant that the two low-key engines of 250 and 300bhp were quieter and more gentle, a fact which no doubt was pleasing to the largest percentage of buyers who opted for greater comfort of these two alternatives.

But at exactly the same moment, and no doubt as pleasing to the hot-shoes on the street, the two firebreathers were given new valves and ports, as well as a new cam to replace the evergreen Duntov grind which had lasted so well since 1956. Also new, from the plant at Muncie, Indiana, was a four-speed manual transmission which was light, positive, and very effective. This was to be the most powerful format in which Chevrolet ever offered the 327bhp smallblock, extracting a massive 375bhp at 6200rpm and 350lbs/ft of torque at 4600rpm.

The Press received the new model with great enthusiasm. *Car Life*, who had given the 1963 their award for engineering excellence the year before, were so impressed with the 1964 and so disappointed with everything else that they made no award at all in 1964. The Sting Ray was, impossible as it may have seemed after the acclaim accorded to the 1963 model, getting better and better.

And even while improvements to the current model were being enthused over by Press and buyers alike, the GM design staff were already prepared for the next major body changes, and at the end of 1964 had got as far as a full-size clay mockup of the next step. This model, which wasn't destined to see the light of day on the production line until 1968, would have looked remarkably familiar to present owners of current models right up to 1982.

So for 1965 the changes were confined to small restyles on the existing body shape. The hood louvers were scrapped entirely, remaining only as

Previous pages: All change again: the new Corvette for 1968, a style that stayed with the car until 1983.

Above: The crossed flags nose badge, current from 1964 through 1967.

Left: The 1963 Corvette brought in the electrically-operated hidden headlights that have characterized the car ever since. For 1964 they moved over to metal housings. They were fiberglass in 1963.

Above right: In 1964, a base Corvette Sports Coupe would have set you back $4522. By 1967 it was only $4388.

Right: The 1964 Coupes differ almost only in the rear screen. Yet collectors will always prefer the 1963, and values reflect this.

Left: By 1965 Corvette had the 327ci V8 with 250bhp, but it was also the first year of the 425HP 396ci big-block option.

Right: A Nassau Blue 1965 Coupe with the optional finned cast aluminum knock-off wheels.

Below: The Convertible was always the cheaper of the two models. In 1965 it was more than $200 cheaper at $4106.

embryonic depressions either side of the familiar central bulge in the hood which is still a feature of Corvette styling.

Also still a feature of the current Corvette was the introduction for 1965 of all-round disk brakes, an event greeted with sighs of relief from those quarters which had been expecting their arrival for some years. Indeed most people felt that Corvette should have had disks years before 1965, a point which Duntov has since conceded. There was a certain amount of feeling prevalent at the time which said that any performance car worthy of the name ought necessarily to be equipped with disk brakes, at least at the front, if not all round. Performance cars are, after all, designed to be at the forefront of motoring technology rather than lagging about five years behind.

But although this was true, and although the pressure on GM to fit disks was enormous, the situation wasn't that simple, nor was it one which Chevrolet had been ignoring. In fact the Grand Sport Corvettes which ran through the 1963 race season had indeed been fitted with Girling disk brakes, but although these had proved entirely adequate for the lightweight race cars they were totally unsuitable for the 1000lbs of extra weight which the production models carried around. But having used them successfully on the race cars, Girling set out with complete confidence to design a braking system for the production car – and failed.

The whole Corvette ethos was one of design and engineering excellence, preferably with a well-proven track record, and Duntov was unwilling to put on disks just so that Chevrolet could say they were fitted to Corvette. In any case there was very little wrong with the massive drum brakes already fitted. Admittedly they could be harsh, even brutal, in operation, and there was no doubt that disks would provide a much more civilized feel to the driver, but the drums had tested out tremendously well. The 1964 model, tested by *Car Life*, had excelled in the brake tests to the point where the testers had abandoned their usual emergency stops from 80mph and piled straight in with crash stops first from 100mph and then from 110 and again from 100. The third test, giving a time fractionally over 20 seconds, was 'better by far than anything we have ever tested.'

It would be a brave engineer indeed (or a foolish marketing executive) who would be prepared to sacrifice that advantage simply to gain the appeal of disk brakes. After Girling's failure to come up with the right answer, development work on disk brakes for Corvette was transferred to GM's own Delco subsidiary. Duntov, after much testing, was convinced that, in order to obtain the results he wanted, disk brakes would have to be power-assisted, but this had been vetoed by the accountants, once again purely on the grounds of economic realities.

MUSCLECAR: THE BIG BLOCK YEARS 69

70 MUSCLECAR: THE BIG BLOCK YEARS

Delco went ahead on an unboosted system more or less based on that which Girling had tried to get right themselves. This was a split-caliper arrangement which is standard on all disks almost without exception today, using two cylinders either side of the disk and a facility for simple withdrawal of the pads from behind with minimum effort.

Delco differed from Girling and everybody else in the auto industry in abandoning the principle of positive withdrawal of the pads. This system involves the mechanical retraction of the braking pads from the disks after the braking application has ended. Delco ignored this, and let their pads rest permanently but gently against the disk, allowing almost instant pedal response and making the brakes almost impervious to rain and ice.

Braking experts had previously scorned this idea on the basis that the pads would continually wear themselves out while at the same time providing a friction against the motion of the car; they said that, in effect, the brakes would be slightly on all the time. This latter effect was never noticed, but the problem of pad wear was, and Delco went through 127 different compounds before they found the right one, and braking tests on the road were commenced.

Brake testing was then conducted on a tortuous road course in very hilly country in Virginia and it was to this proving route that the Corvette equipped with experimental disks was taken. After a lot of high-speed driving, stopping and starting to a point well beyond what Chevrolet brake specialist Arnold Brown described as 'the idiot limit' he reported that 'no significant data' had been obtained. The car had outbraked the test route, and a special brake abuse course had to be created just to take Corvette's disk system to its limit and back.

In 1965 Corvette was offered with four-wheel disks for the first time, disks which were 'totally free from fade' and hauled the car down from frighteningly high speeds in frighteningly short times in dead straight lines. So effective were the brakes that *Road and Track* claimed that they were 'boring.'

It was indeed fortunate that the disk system was sorted out when it was, because it wasn't the only surprise in the Chevrolet portfolio for 1965, and it is quite likely that the other one would have been fatal for most Corvette owners without the first.

Following the introduction of the smallblock V8, Chevrolet had backed it up later with the big-block, although naturally enough the smallblock wasn't called the smallblock until after the big-block came out and made it so. This bigger engine, at 396ci, was used for passenger sedans alone, although it

Far left: Trunk/hood badge gives you the name.

Left: Front fender badge gives you the company. Injected cars had a further script underneath.

Below left: Post-1967 styling was low and swoopy, but for many enthusiasts lacked the character of the earlier cars. Stingray was one word by now.

Right: For 1965 the 300HP 327ci smallblock was just one of six engine choices.

had also provided sterling service on the racetrack as a stock car engine. Duntov had never seen the use of the big-block in the Corvette as a viable proposition, mostly because of the inherent weight problem with all that ironwork, and had consequently striven to get the maximum output from the much handier 327ci unit.

But as the cries for simple brute power became louder and other makers turned out their musclecars it became clear that Corvette would have to offer a big-inch option.

The bottom end of the passenger car ('W') engine was used for this, together with a new top end developed for the stock car circuits. The unusual valve arrangement, which left the top of the head with a mess of valves sticking up all over instead of in straight lines, caused it to be known as a porcupine head. This strange classification resulted in the big-block engine being known as the rat motor (since porcupines are only a spiky kind of rodent) and the smallblock then being christened the 'mouse motor.'

The arrival of the big-block into the Corvette body was more or less inevitable. At the tail end of 1962 ace race engineer Mickey Thompson had already put one into one of the first Sting Rays available, with dramatic results, so it was only a question of time before it became a factory option.

When it came, the 396 had an 11:1 compression ratio, solid lifters, and a single four-barrel Holley carburetor. The 327ci engine, maximum rating, had produced 365bhp with fuel injection. In stock carbureted form the 396 was quoted at 425bhp. Straight out of the crate and blueprinted, one had delivered 442bhp. This was definitely what they wanted.

Aside from disks, the big-block Sting Ray also acquired stiffer front springs to carry the extra weight, together with thick rollbars front and rear. With that done, and all the weight up front, the ratio had only changed very slightly from the smallblock-equipped Sting Ray – 51 front, 49 rear. Better still, there was little or no appreciable change in the entirely satisfactory handling characteristics introduced the previous year.

From outside, the car needed a large hood bulge in order to conceal the top of the taller big-block engine, which gave it a menacing appeal that quite suited the mood of the time. On top of this, and to the enormous delight of almost everyone (if current press cuttings are to be believed), the car also grew sidepipes; chromed external four-into-one headers leading into a huge fluted chrome muffler pipe which ran the entire length of the car between front and rear wheels.

This shining monstrosity was universally admired, despite the fact that everybody burned their leg on it sooner or later; again it was completely symptomatic of the era and was fortunately a victim of increasingly stringent motoring laws which led to its eventual demise in 1970.

The car changed little in appearance for 1966; the revamped body wasn't ready for the street yet, although it had been patrolling around under the guise of the Mako Shark showcar for quite some while, and had even got into Shark Mark II form.

In 1966 Corvette dropped fuel injection, the bolt-on option which had been solely responsible for making the 327ci a race engine instead of a street engine all those years ago. The reasoning, according to Chevrolet, was simply that the injection system cost an extra $538 while the most expensive and most powerful engine option only added $313 to the base price of the car.

But power news for this year came in the form of the bored-out big-block, the largest engine yet offered. The machining lost 30 cubic inches of metal, and the 427ci accelerated the Sting Ray from rest to 60mph in about five seconds, maybe less with a clever driver. Quarter-mile times stayed in much the same area as they'd always been – high 13, low 14 and about 100mph – while the maximum was in the area of 150mph depending on your luck and the local police.

In this form the Sting Ray was far faster than every other production car America had to offer. Its superior chassis and suspension meant that it could not only outgun them on paper but also out-handle them on the corners too. Now that the back end was sorted out with IRS it could lay all of its power on the tarmac smoothly and easily, charging off towards its phenomenal top speed while other contenders like the Pontiac GTO sat still and went up in smoke, tires spinning uselessly on the spot. The only domestic car which could give the Sting Ray a hard time was the 427 Cobra, and their complete lack of comfort or weather protection meant that the few of them which existed spent most of their time in garages; when they did get used in anger it was generally on a racetrack and not on the street.

By 1967 the situation was settled. The Corvette was a winner at just about every level as far as sportscars were concerned. Styling was still unchanged and not yet dated – it had few competitors in any case, and none anywhere near as good looking – and the slight engine variations were even a further improvement on previous years. Strangely enough the new carburation

MUSCLECAR: THE BIG BLOCK YEARS

Left: A 1966 Convertible with optional big-block power. The 427ci engined cars have the extra wide hood bulge.

Right: And this is what it looks like under the hood. The massive 427ci big block V8 in a 1966.

Below: 1967s are considered the smoothest of all the early models, as they lost some of the badges and gained the neater side fins. Side mount exhaust system was optional at $131.

setup, using three two-barrel Holleys, offered such a smooth and progressive power take-up that yet again the press enthused and the boulevard cruisers swarmed into the showrooms to get their hands on one of the 20,000-plus models sold that year.

The streetracers were far from disappointed with the almost traditional annual step forward made with the Chevrolet V8. For 1967 the go-faster innovation was the final arrival of aluminum heads; the L88 motor came with a 12.5:1 compression ratio and a single 850cfm Holley sitting on an alloy manifold. This monster produced a tremendous 560bhp at 6400rpm and could only be obtained as part of a total package order in which the car came without heater and screen defroster in an attempt to discourage its use on the street; it was quite simply a full-house race car straight from the factory production line.

And it was busy proving it, too. Although Corvettes were still having trouble with the super-light Cobras in short-distance SCCA races they were more than proving their value over longer distances at Sebring, Daytona, and now even at Le Mans. At the 1967 24 hours race the Sting Ray, by 300lbs the heaviest car in its class, led for 11½ hours before the L88 finally did what so many of them were prone to do and blew up completely. But for those 11 hours the Corvette had shown its heels to every car in its class. The next fastest contender had been a Ferrari which was a full 20mph slower than the Corvette's 170mph along the Mulsanne straight and eventually won.

Even that wasn't the peak for the year; at Bonneville a 427ci Corvette with Hillborn fuel injection won with a recorded top speed of 192mph.

In many ways 1968 was a year of change. Progress is endemic to technology; the minute it stands still it's dead, and it's something which has always been reflected by the consumer demanding the most up-to-date product available, an attitude which is never more noticeable than in automobile styling. The point has been made before; car makers have to update their models every year, even if doing so effects no useful changes whatever.

At the forefront of car styling comes the sportscar, and change, to demonstrate an awareness of technical advance and make it available to the buyers in the technically snobbish world of performance motoring, is the very lifeblood of the industry.

Fortunately for Chevrolet their involvement in racing – albeit highly unofficial – what with the various show and research vehicles like CERV and the Mako Shark, had meant that they were as far ahead in conceptual thinking as anyone else. However, big company politics and organization don't always lend themselves to rapid advances on the production line.

MUSCLECAR: THE BIG BLOCK YEARS   75

Left: The 1967 Corvette had much of the 1968 car's new developments but the old body. The new hood had the giant built-in scoop.

Above: The L72 engine option. For 1966 only you could have this 427ci motor with 425bhp at 6400rpm.

Above right: The Sting Ray got its name and most of its styling from the Mitchell race car.

Right: Vettes just don't look the same with the lights flipped up.

MUSCLECAR: THE BIG BLOCK YEARS 77

Above left: The 1967 interior is distinguishable by the position of the handbrake — between the seats at last.

Left: Marlboro Maroon brings out the chiseled lines of this 1967.

Above: Because it was virtually the 1968 car with the old body, the 1967s have the advantage over the early Sting Rays in features like four-way flashers, dual master cylinders, and six-inch rims.

Right: Stock engine for 1967 was the 300HP 327ci unit with a 10.25:1 compression ratio.

Left: The 1968 Corvette met with so many complaints in the areas of design and quality control that *Car and Driver* magazine claimed it wasn't even good enough to warrant a test.

Right: Chevrolet dropped the Sting Ray name for 1968, but brought it back as Stingray in 1969. This 1968 looks almost plain after the chrome trim of the earlier models.

While the smaller specialist firms in Europe, like Ferrari, were able to halt short production runs to make minor or even major changes very swiftly, the same was never true of the GM monolith. More to the point, Ferrari have never had to worry about amortizing the cost of retooling for such changes over any great period of time; people expect to pay a great deal for technical excellence and they expect to pay even more for it when it wears a prancing horse on the hood. Ferrari have never experienced the same resistance to price that volume-production manufacturers have to face every day.

For the economics of Corvette to make any sense at all to the cold-blooded accountants of a large company there was little chance of Corvette making radical changes every year, even though Corvette engineering were aware of every advance and generally almost ready to produce it; time after time it was an iron grip on the purse-strings which prevented such advances.

As far as GM were concerned Corvette, even running at more than 20,000 units per year, was a low-volume car; to make itself in any way contributory and not become an expensive luxury, it was essential that basic parts — chassis, body, and engine — remain in production for as long as possible in order that a certain amount of profit could be made. In its entire lifetime of 30 years Corvette has seen very few major changes of body or chassis, even suspension. Even the 350ci V8 which powers it today derives directly from the 283ci unit which appeared in 1955. This was the only way that GM could make money and keep the car in production this long.

In the light of this sort of handicap, coupled with the political infighting which is the hallmark of all large corporations, it is a tribute to those people most closely concerned that Corvette has not only survived, but has consistently been refined over the years, and remained true to its original ethos. This continuing search for perfection balanced against financial viability could have led to unfortunate compromise more than once. It is again a tribute to the engineering skills of those involved that such compromise has never been made to the detriment of the car on the road as it existed, although it has affected what might have been very greatly.

With this in mind it is not difficult to admire Duntov's courage in delaying the introduction of the major restyle scheduled for Corvette in 1967 for a further year, in order that as many of the last-minute difficulties as possible could be ironed out and the car could be the best that could be made rather than simply adequate.

Towards the end of the sixties, Corvette was entering a difficult period in its life, perhaps even more troublesome than the early years when it looked as if the red pen of accountancy would strike it down. During an era of rapid technological change it had remained basically the same since 1963. Having swept Ford's Thunderbird under the carpet it was once again facing heavy competition, a great deal of it from within GM. This competition can perhaps best be personified by the Camaro; a sporty two-plus-two which drew heavily on GM experience with manufacture and marketing of Corvette, which didn't have the shattering performance of the Sting Ray but which didn't cost as much either.

Knowing that the future was far from assured, GM were working towards a redesign in two areas. The main styling house was looking once again towards a rear-engined car. Their concept was, like the Corvair, a water-cooled V8 mounted behind the back axle line on a backbone chassis.

This concept suffered badly in one major area — handling. Whenever things got difficult the huge mass of engine at the rear took over from the driver, and the car demonstrated a distinct tendency for the rear wheels to overtake the front in fast cornering. If that wasn't bad enough it got worse in the wet, and did the same thing at low speed. Not even a huge bias towards over-wide rear tires could overcome this problem, and it seemed insoluble.

Meanwhile Duntov was trying out ideas on a similar basis, except that his project was more mid-engined than rear-engined. The V8 sat ahead of the axle line in a 99-inch chassis, a combination which showed much better handling properties and is still in widespread use. However the cost of tooling up for the transaxle setup needed for this arrangement was totally prohibitive, running into millions of dollars.

Both departments were working along very similar lines for the body-styling, and both owed a great deal to the Mako Shark showcar which had been touring since 1965. Aerodynamically smooth, everything on the Shark was recessed, rising from the body at the touch of a vacuum switch — wipers, front lamps, rear lights — and it was more of a Corvette-like projectile than an automobile.

With this as a base, Duntov's body for the facelift incorporated a steel insert to back the passenger compartment, giving a rollover protection bar across the top and allowing the roof to be lifted off, turning hardtop coupe into convertible in one easy move. The recessed rear window could also be clipped out to emphasize this effect.

Styling had also come up with a similar-looking concept which featured a solid roof accommodating gullwing doors, a huge wraparound windshield, rear fender skirts, and no rear screen whatever, but using a periscope for rearward vision. Their project died the death as well, like the Q-car and like Duntov's mid-engined prototype, when the huge cost of tooling for the transaxle became apparent, and there seemed to be no new shape for Corvette forthcoming from either direction.

But there was on the stocks yet another theme car which had been created more or less as a functional, production version of the Mako Shark. Without all the high-technology, this one retained the outward appearance, somewhat toned down, of the Shark, was V8 powered, and used the existing front-engine chassis.

This theme car was the only option available and it was on this that the revamped Corvette was based. From Corvette engineering it went, as usual, to styling for the final production touches to be added and was then used as an aerodynamic testbed to make sure it had all the desirable qualities.

In testing it was compared against the 1965 body style and it came off rather badly. Tests were conducted at 120mph, which was the control speed for just about everything connected with Corvette, since it was in this

80 MUSCLECAR: THE BIG BLOCK YEARS

Left: 1968 was different in so many ways. The Coupe now featured a T-top arrangement with two removable roof panels and a rear window which also came out.

Below: It's interesting how little American interior trim has changed since this 1968. The seats were the most raked yet to take in the steeply laid-back windshield.

Right: Chevrolet changed the names of their colors almost every year. This is Silverstone Silver.

general area of the speedometer that Duntov believed most owners wished to travel and that design work should therefore be centred around it to cater for them, rather than at a lower speed.

The 1965 body needed 155bhp to move it at 120mph, at which speed the body lifted 2¾ inches at the front and ½ inch at the rear. The new body had a lip spoiler at the back and this was expected to change the situation somewhat. It did, but the rest of the body changed it even more. At 120mph the front lifted by an extra quarter-inch and the rear was pressed down by a quarter, which didn't sound too bad. But the new shape required 210bhp to move it along at 120mph, a situation which could hardly have been much worse.

Fortunately for Corvette, Chevrolet had not stayed out of motor racing entirely, as anyone who has watched the success of the Chaparral team will know. Chaparral were the first to use an adjustable rear spoiler long before the rear wings became a common sight on the racetrack.

Drawing heavily on their expertise gained with Chaparral, the new-shape Corvette gained a chin spoiler across the front and vents in the front fenders from which airflow could exit cleanly without building up pressure beneath the body. Both of these innovations had already been tried with success on Chaparral race cars.

Cutting the vents in the fender reduced the horsepower required at 120mph from 210 to 175. The chin spoiler reduced the requirement even

Left: Believe it or not, front bumper height was reduced for the 1968 models. Headlights were now vacuum-operated and popped up instead of swiveling as before.

Below right: 1968 was the last year of the 327ci smallblock, as the 350ci unit was about to take over.

further – to 105, while with both in place the body lift was now down to about half an inch at the front.

The situation seemed perfect and all was set for the new shape to be launched in 1967, but Duntov was still not happy. He was worried about the lack of vision available to the driver in the new body. Hi-rise fenders at the front obstructed the view all round, while the rear spoiler and enclosed flat window arrangement, with long backward-sloping quarter-panels, restricted the view through the mirror or while backing up to a dramatic extent.

It was his persuasion that caused GM to hold the new shape over for yet another year at a time when all other cars were getting annual facelifts, and the ghost of Carroll Hall Shelby came back to haunt them as Ford announced the Shelby Cobra Mustangs in GT 350 or GT 500 versions; the competition had never been as stiff as it was now, but Duntov and his team didn't want to compromise the future by putting out a car which was, in their opinion, not as it should have been.

In the breathing space they had gained by deferring the launch most of the problems with the new body were sorted easily enough. The front fenders were reduced in height as much as was possible (allowing for wheel travel) – to give the driver some chance of seeing what was going on ahead, and the line of the rear fenders was also slightly changed to help with the backing up view. The line of the quarter panels down from the roof to the edge of the rear fenders was also changed, and the once-parabolic scoop became flatter and more businesslike. The rear spoiler, which had proved almost unnecessary in tests anyway, was almost completely gone, leaving only an embryonic curl across the lip of the rear deck, and with that done the all-round vision was a good as it was ever going to be.

Drivers of the pre-1984 Corvettes will already know that despite all this the raised hackle of the front fender gets in the way a great deal as far as front threequarter vision is concerned, especially toward the passenger side. This can create problems when maneuvering in traffic or parking to begin with; but it takes only a very short while before a sense of size and location of those parts of the car invisible from the driving seat grows. In any case, if it came to a straight choice between vision and the satisfying, attacking humps of the front fenders, almost up to the driver's eyeline, 100 Corvette owners out of 100 would go for the fenders, not the vision.

With all that sorted there was still one remaining problem – the removable top. Body flexing on the road made it noisy, drafty, wet, and unreliable, and no practical amount of stiffening could overcome it. In the end the roof was split into halves and taken off in two parts, and the ubiquitous T-top was born, although only just, because this modification was made so late that production had to be delayed to accommodate it.

Less trouble than the roof were the pop-up lights, now powered by a vacuum system, which has always seemed to give less trouble than electrically-raised lights. Also vacuum powered was the shield over the recessed wipers, an idea which came directly from the super-smooth Shark. Also a direct inheritance from the same benefactor were the improved interior ventilation and the use of fiber optics to convey information to the dashboard about the conditon of all the vehicle lighting systems.

The only problem on the new shape which remained unsolved was the cooling. The all-enclosing shroud of the new body gave the engine a distinct and unpleasant tendency to overheat under anything but the most ideal conditions. Idling, heavy traffic or steep hills were enough to create chaos in the coolant in very short order, something which was even more pronounced in cars with the big engine options.

Before he had a chance to sort this problem out properly, Duntov was taken ill and admitted to hospital. When he was discharged the car was almost ready for full production and a press preview – using one car with a big-block engine – was imminent. Last minute panic was called for, and Duntov was forced to work fast. A makeshift extension to the chin spoiler forced cold air upwards and into extra ducting in the grille which Duntov cut himself. Having got air into the car he then sealed off all exits except one – the radiator core – and forced the air through it.

There wasn't time to test this arrangement properly and it was left to the press to find out whether or not it worked. On the day, amid crossed fingers and pleading eyes raised to the heavens, it came out all right. The big engine ran on the hot side of normal, but it was felt that this was about the best that could be hoped for, and overheating has always been a problem for this model, even with Duntov's extras added to production-line units.

The overall shape of this car was the best yet. In a word it was stunning. It was everything a sports car should be; sleek, long, lean, low, and positively hungry-looking, just waiting for some impudent boulevard cruiser to snap up as an *hors d'oeuvre* before winding itself rapidly up to its massive top speed.

Here again, though, there were contradictions. The lowering of the hood to help forward vision had meant that the manifold needed to be redesigned in order to get the carburetors in under the hood. In itself this didn't detract from performance, but the new hood fitted to the L88-engined models drew cold air in from the dead area below the windshield, which Duntov tested as reducing the acceleration performance drastically. The L88 version now took seven seconds longer to reach 140mph, although top speed remained more or less the same – up from 183 to 185mph.

In view of the fact that the body now weighed 100lbs more than the previous shape – most of which was in the extra seven-inch front overhang, things weren't all bad. With the roofline lowered by two inches and the width increased as well, the shape conspired to be the most dramatic-looking Corvette yet, with an appearance rivalling and equalling the most exotic vehicles which the Italian specialist coachbuilders had yet turned out.

On paper and in testing programs it seemed very clear that the Corvette team had done it again; facelifted an old friend while making certain that it retained all of its character and more, while yet again taking a few more steps toward the kind of performance and handling which would be beyond the psychological limits of all but a very few of those who drove it.

But while Duntov had been ill the struggle for control of Corvette which had been continuing for some while seemed to have been lost, and the car had been almost completely absorbed into the maw of the GM giant. Launched in 1968 (without the Sting Ray appellation which had been its touchstone for so long), Corvette was now being treated as just another production model, and somehow all of Duntov's 'special' authority over the car had been whittled away to almost nothing, as he was posted away into the backwoods of engineering research.

Corvette, though, honed in the rough and tumble world of the race track, learning its lessons at Sebring, Daytona, Bonneville, and Le Mans at the very limits of engineering skill and tuning, was not a car which could be treated as just another production model, and it very soon demonstrated this fact to almost everyone who chose to sit in it during that first facelift year.

The main problem seemed to be one of quality control, which manifested itself via a staggering multitude and variety of niggling faults. The clip-on roof leaked, the sound-deadening was horrifically bad, the body panels rattled and creaked and groaned, they grated against each other where they butted up (in the few places they actually did), and all manner of bits and pieces fell off. It was a deplorable situation.

The biggest single blow came while Duntov was in Europe, showing the car to a European press who received it quite well, despite its drawbacks. *Car and Driver*, given a new Corvette for road test, refused point blank to do so, and went to great lengths in their pages to say that they had found it 'unfit' and then to list all of the 49-plus things which were wrong with it after only a few miles. They weren't the only people who felt that way; other magazines, and a great number of new owners, shared their views and lost no time in saying so as publicly as possible. For Chevrolet the problem was one of paradox: how to treat as a volume production model a highly-specialized thoroughbred sportscar? For the answer to this question they turned once again to the man who had been solving the problem for them over the past ten years or more, and Zora Duntov returned to Corvette as Chief Engineer.

Later in the same year *Car and Driver* were supplied with one of Duntov's test models and were forced to agree with his prognosis, that this was 'the best Corvette ever.' *Road & Track* and *Car Life* also agreed, 'If all you want,' said *Road & Track*, 'is blinding acceleration – buy one.'

As if to prove a point, Corvette took to the racetrack again after Chevrolet had told the FIA that they had built 500 L88 hardtops and gained homologation. This statement wasn't a little white lie. It was a big fat black one, since (according to Karl Ludvigsen, author of *Corvette – America's Star-spangled Sportscar*) no such cars existed at all, but the few that found their way onto the track in later months beat all the opposition in sight, including the few fading Cobras. Anyway, it followed a long and dishonorable tradition in the annals of motorsport, which perhaps signalled that on the world's most prestigious racetracks and among the glitter of the most historic names in the racing world, Corvette was no different from anyone else.

Under Attack: Surviving the Fuel Crisis

86 UNDER ATTACK: SURVIVING THE FUEL CRISIS

In a way, 1969 was almost the last year that everything went absolutely right for Corvette. If ever a car could be said to have a heyday then for Corvette it was 1969. With the turn of the decade the first signs of the coming crisis started to appear, but just for now everything was tinged with a golden glow.

Sales of Corvette had been pushing steadily upward ever since Job One; each year had seen more units of Chevrolet's most glamorous (and now most expensive) model hit the streets. 1968 had closed with more than 28,000 of them sold. 1969 looked all set to be yet another record year.

As ever in auto manufacture, the pressure to get a new model into production had been truly enormous, and despite the year of respite which Duntov had gained for Corvette, the 1968 model was not yet the full realization of the car's true potential. There is a maxim among the car-buying public which warns against buying a new model in its first year, and dictates that those with any sense will hold back. Let the poseurs and the snobs rush in where angels fear to tread, it goes, and then next year, when they have paid the price of the teething problems in a full measure of aggravation, we can step in and buy the new car trouble-free.

In the case of the 1968 relaunch this adage has never been more true, and it wasn't until very late in the year that the St Louis plant began to get on top of the production snags and again turn out cars of which they could justifiably be proud. On top of this there was a whole rash of minor changes to the 1969 car which are in many cases so trivial as to seem pointless. If nothing else they serve as a pointer to the enormous number of minor headaches which owners of the new model had been forced to tolerate during the initial year. All these changes combine to become the closest thing to an admission of guilt which a car manufacturer is ever likely to make.

But with Duntov back at the helm all of them received attention and all of the things which were wrong with the 1968 (but shouldn't have been) were sorted for 1969. In a kind of re-affirmation of faith in the new year's production run, Corvette once again bore the hallowed script. Condensed to just one word, the name Stingray came back to the street.

The biggest change on the line was the shift to eight-inch wheels, something which demonstrated once again the uncompromising attitude held by the Corvette team at the time. Wheels of this width belong in truth on a racetrack but not on the street. They improve handling no end at higher speed, but make the car a great deal less pleasant to be in at lower speeds. But the whole of Corvette's suspension and chassis has always been engineered to produce its best response in the bracket between 80 and 120mph. Although perhaps the major percentage of owners seldom use or appreciate this fact – as witnessed by the large numbers going for the soft-option engines as opposed to the more powerful variants – Duntov always believed that his responsibility was to those who wanted to drive quickly; something Corvette has always been about.

Almost in direct contradiction of this attitude, GM started to speak of the car as a luxury sportster, a phrase more than passingly redolent of the old

Previous pages: After 1974 Corvettes came with the impact-absorbing rear section in the body color. In 1975 they also added the little bumper pads to the nose section.

Above: The 1969 Corvette. Stingray badge, but no wheelarch flares until 1970.

Left: 1969 is still considered in many ways the last of the golden years as a combination of oil crisis and government regulations against muscle cars was about to bite.

Ford compromise, the 'personal' Thunderbird. It was during this period that Corvette began to grow what *Car and Driver* later described as its 'life of Riley appurtenances,' starting simply with inertia reel seatbelts and moving drastically to a proliferation of warning lights which blinked at the pilot if the doors were ajar, the headlights only partially open, or if any number of other marginally relevant happenings were afoot. New for 1969 was a dash plaque which proclaimed the nature of the engine fitted to the beast, something which indeed bespoke the individual care and attention which the cars were given on the St Louis line. More importantly, and adding the kind of detail touch which one may perhaps be entitled to expect on an expensive exoticar but could not rightfully demand from a giant like GM, were the tachometers. All the different engine variations had a different redline, and each car bore a tacho appropriately marked for the engine beneath the hood. It was this kind of detail which was destined to disappear once the auto industry discovered the meaning of the word 'rationalization.'

Also soon to meet that same ax was the huge choice of just about everything else. Cars were built almost completely to the specifications of individual buyers, right down to axle ratios. Corvette was offered, in 1969, with several, including the drag-racing-only 4.56:1, even though only 20 vehicles were built with this installed from the tens of thousands which came off the line in that year.

Big news for smallblock buyers was that once again Chevrolet had increased the capacity of the engine, lifting it to 350ci – in which form it has now survived as the only engine option for Corvette. This engine created a maximum of 300bhp at 4800rpm in standard base trim, but with 11:1 heads it could summon up another 50bhp at 5800rpm.

The most important news of the year was almost certainly in the big-block end of the market. Once again Chevrolet's policy of non-involvement with motor racing had produced another winning combination, this time in conjunction with the McLaren team's assault on the Can-Am series. Using the success of the lightweight aluminum heads which were the base of the L88, GM had produced an all-aluminum block as well. Attached to the heads the combination was designated ZL1 and was the most devastating powerpack they had yet produced, as McLaren's domination in Can-Am proved beyond doubt. Light, but reasonably strong, the ZL1 engine delivered all the punch a racer could ask for, but saved large amounts of weight, making itself not only a powerplant but also an aid to handling as well.

Excellent on the track, the ZL1 was by no stretch of the imagination a street-going motor, and for fast road performance the steel block L88 was still the favorite choice. Both engines used the 'open chamber' head, in which the combustion chamber was opened out towards the plug, which didn't help with the engine's breathing but certainly helped with the burning.

In this form it was highly sensitive, and clearance gaps between head and block were critical, lest heat build-up lead forthwith to outright detonation. This wasn't too much of a problem on the L88, but on the aluminum ZL1, which was prone to a great deal more expansion and contraction in varying temperatures, it could be a major headache. ZL1 engines were always, of necessity, tuned right up to the maximum, something which is not only acceptable, but generally wholly desirable in a race car while remaining a complete nonsense on the street. Both engines produced similar dyno figures, though, which left the ZL1 unchallenged on the track and the L88 in a similar state of mastery as GM's all-steel, all-power road motor.

Even so, Corvette was offered with the ZL1 package. The engines were built slowly and individually in almost surgical conditions, and delivered in Corvettes which, as a no-option part of the package, were devoid of all the refined extras and lacked heater, airconditioning and even power steering, in an attempt to ensure that it was never used on the road. Despite this the ZL1 strangely came with cast-iron manifolding which everybody with any sense at all immediately junked and replaced with headers so that the engine could breathe well enough to deliver all of its promise.

A stock ZL1 Corvette weighed in at a mere 2900lbs and was capable of 12-second quarters, topping out at the far end at about 115mph, although a one-off ZL1, built for drag racing by Chevrolet, pulled 11 seconds and 127mph – back in 1969.

All in all 1969 turned out to be a good year. A two-month strike had held up production severely though, and it was on the orders of John Z DeLorean that the 1969 model year production run, which would normally have terminated in about October, ran on longer, perhaps contributing to the record output for the year. Always on the increase by a few percent every year, Corvette production jumped from 28,000 in 1968 to a massive 38,000 in 1969. It was also in 1969 that GM, in an appropriate blaze of publicity, handed over the keys of Corvette number 250,000 to a buyer in California. Unlike the bulk of the 1969 models (57 percent were the pretty coupes) this one was a convertible.

The longer run for 1969 wasn't the only thing which John DeLorean accomplished. At last, here was a man GM had waited for. Not only did he know what rationalization meant, he also knew how to achieve it. It was also he who pushed Corvette more firmly towards its 'luxury sportster' image, with a subtle dressing-up program which included small changes to the grille and parking lights, tinted glass as standard all round, extra headroom (gained by altering the seats, not the roofline) and a few other minor frills.

It was in 1970 that Corvette had won a *Car and Driver* poll as the most popular car around, and John DeLorean wasn't slow to take advantage of it. Aside from pushing for greater numbers off the production line – a forced march which had already shown itself as being detrimental to the quality of individual cars as a matter of inevitable course, DeLorean was also committing Corvette to a pricing policy which caused a sharp rise in the base price in 1970 and again in 1971. If Corvette was America's most popular car then people were clearly prepared to pay for it, went the reasoning, a state of mind which was totally in opposition to the original thinking behind the Corvette pricing and marketing policy all those forgotten years ago.

Corvette buyers in 1971, if they wanted the civilization they'd shown a preference for in previous years, had to pay a lot for the car and then pay extra for power windows, power steering, power brakes, and a simple FM radio.

As the swinging sixties gradually metamorphosed into the not-so-swinging seventies it was clear that the wind of change was in the air. As Britain discovered her own oil in the North Sea, the growing tide of dissent in the Middle East glared in a worldwide highlight when three hijacked airliners were blown up by extremists in Jordan. Although it was not yet widely evident, the fuel crisis, the environmentalist movement, and the vast number of consumer bodies, spearheaded by Ralph Nader, were sharpening their teeth, ready to plunge them into the succulent and vulnerable flank of the auto industry in an attack which would sound the death knell of the gas-greedy low-volume specialist cars.

As far as styling changes were concerned, the early seventies were, for the most part, fairly lean years. With the introduction of the revised shape in 1968 it seemed that Corvette had extended itself as far as it could go without losing essential features of its character. There is, after all, a limit to how far a body shape can be taken, and Corvette appeared to be there. In any case, basic production economics dictated that the body would have to remain in production for a while longer yet. A glance back into history shows that the first body lasted only three years, while the second one saw a downturn in prosperity in the industry and ran for a comparatively lengthy seven years almost without change. The third shape lasted six years while the fourth, other than a minor cosmetic change after six years, has continued for a staggering fifteen years. Although economics must play their part in this, and although it is often foolish to change a formula which is winning harder now than it was fifteen years ago, it is hard to avoid the suspicion that there isn't anywhere for the body design to go.

In any case, most of the impetus toward change in the automobile industry, especially where specialist cars like Corvette are concerned, has long since been legislated out of existence.

Left: The LT-1 option was the solid lifter, 370HP 350ci smallblock, nearly as powerful as the LS5 454ci big block.

Top right and right: For 1970, Corvette still had the chrome bumpers but the grilles were different. There were new front turn signals too.

Overleaf: A rare 1970 complete with LT-1. The 1970 saw few real external changes.

UNDER ATTACK: SURVIVING THE FUEL CRISIS 89

92 UNDER ATTACK: SURVIVING THE FUEL CRISIS

UNDER ATTACK: SURVIVING THE FUEL CRISIS

The signs were all there in 1970. It was that year in which the monstrous and biggest-ever 454ci engine was offered as an option on the Corvette. Duntov is said to have claimed that the reason for the overbore was weight saving, and that the absence of the extra inches of cast iron improved handling. Under the circumstances, joking was perhaps his best alternative, since the real reason lay much deeper and darker.

Far from signalling the high point of the musclecar era, the arrival of the big 454ci unit was the sign that their days were numbered, even though their place in legend may well have been assured. It is sad but true that the 454 was less powerful than its smaller predecessor, the 427, when in road trim. The 427ci unit delivered 435 bhp at 5800rpm, the 454ci only 390bhp at 4800 rpm. Multiplying emission control legislation was at the root of all this. In 1964 Chevrolet had been running a positive crankcase ventilation system which had been uprated to air injection by 1966 and had escalated to full catalytic converter systems by 1975. As everyone now knows full well, these arrangements were gradually choking the life out of the musclecar motors and reducing them to little more than family saloons with a past.

Coupled with this came the certainty that very soon the anti-pollution lobby would have arranged that lead-free gasoline become the order of the day, which would kill off the performance engines without the help of on-board emission control equipment.

The L88 engine, in order to work properly, needed to be fed an octane-rich diet of research or aviation gas; around 103 octane was desirable. Gasoline being what it is, and internal combustion engines being what they are, the only way that powerplants could survive such a mixture was with a plentiful helping of anti-knock ingredients which include large quantities of lead. The future, revolving around lead-free gas, would mean that nothing over 91 octane would be available at the pumps. High-compression engines added to low-octane gas equal very loud explosions.

Insisting that this was going to be a definite part of the future, GM began to lower compression ratios and adjust the timing of their engines during 1970. With all attention devoted to this cause there was little room for work to continue on Corvette as a concept, and development of such a potentially anti-social monster was, in any case, a topic which attracted frowns of disapproval rather than any applause by now.

It was this change in attitude which killed off the natural successor to all the previous freeway-gobbling engines, the LS7 version of the 454ci engine. In LS7 trim this one would have been a monster. It would also have needed 103 octane gas as a very minimum and thus died stillborn before it ever had

Left: The 1971 Coupe with T-top and, if you look closely enough, a luggage rack on the rear deck. These weren't standard but became popular because the limited Corvette luggage space was only accessible from behind the seat.

Below: Chrome egg-crate grilles were a feature of the 1970-72 cars.

96 UNDER ATTACK: SURVIVING THE FUEL CRISIS

a chance. This meant that the only potent option for the seventies was the LS6 motor, bearing the aluminum heads which had been the trademark of the L88, but even that was fairly gutless by comparison to what had been and what could have been.

As a small compensation, the lack of change to the car for 1970 and 1971 meant that there was time available to make the best of it. Further, 1970 was a short production year because of the overrun at the end of 1969; only slightly more than 17,000 units compared to the previous 38,000. Taking advantage of the comparative lull, John DeLorean took some fairly comprehensive steps towards eradicating as many of the production-line problems which had been hanging like a dark cloud over Corvette since 1968 as he could.

And in a further attempt to get away from the reputation for poor quality which had cursed the car over the previous couple of years, he instigated a lengthy and rigorous post-production test program designed to spot all the faults which had been annoying Corvette purchasers over the same period. Included in this, and as a direct result of both rationalization and the growing cloud of fuel shortages, the number of option packages open to Corvette buyers was also drastically reduced. It was during this period that Corvette ceased to be the almost hand-built one-off to customer order which it had become, and fell gradually back into the ranks of production autos.

In 1972 Corvette was offered for sale with only three engine options, the smallest number since 1963, when it had just been growing its reputation. Duntov's ideal of a showroom car which could be driven happily on the street or raced fiercely on the track according to the buyer's whim was receding further and further into the distance.

The sorry tale is illustrated graphically by glancing at the rated outputs of the engines, although a measure of circumspection has to be employed. In an attempt to satisfy the demands of the environmental lobby many Detroit factories had taken to quoting diminished output figures for their bigger engines in the hope that it would provide a *placebo* strong enough to keep the wolf from the door just a little while longer. The big Plymouths – Superbirds – were a prime example. They and not a few other cars were equipped with huge and ridiculously powerful engines, and even hesitant applications of throttle made them almost impossible to drive in a straight line, but the horsepower figures given by the manufacturer were minimized in order to delay the inevitable, and also help owners get insurance for them.

Chevrolet followed a similar policy, although it wasn't quite as blatant, nor as dishonest. In the past all their bhp figures, rounded up to the nearest convenient number, had been established on blueprinted engines with no ancillaries, running on open headers and breathing cold, dense air. Timed up almost to explosive conditions, this arrangement optimized the result and gave the highest possible figure at a time when big number horsepower-ratings were desirable. From now on the opposite was the case, and all the bhp figures quoted were measured at the back wheels of a fully-equipped road car rather than at the flywheel of an almost full-race specification bare engine. This gave them a much greater relevance to the buyer, since they were now much more an indication of the power he had got rather than of the power he could have if he was prepared to make some changes under the hood.

Because of this there is a drastic step downward in quoted power output about now, for all cars and not just Corvette, but even remembering this it is still possible to chart the progress of the sharp knife of emission control as it makes its way across the yearbooks.

The 350ci engine (which is all you can have these days anyway) serves as a useful example. Available in two states of tune, the low-compression L48 and the higher (but hardly, at 9:1, high) compression L82, it has gradually lost most of its tremendous power availability, although it is still in there somewhere, waiting for the drag racer or hotrodder to unlock it, which is why it is still the most popular performance engine in the world.

In 1971 Chevrolet let the 350 out at 330bhp. By 1972 it was down to 255, by 1976 (after the advent of catalytic converters) it was down again to 210 and in 1978 it was rated at a miserable 165bhp. In the same year even the L82 could only struggle through the maze of emission control devices it now wore to produce 205bhp, down from a respectable, if not nerve-shattering 330 in 1971.

Even the mighty 454ci unit, introduced in 1970 with a comfortable 390bhp (still well down on the 435 of the previous year's 427) was phased out of Corvette options in 1974, suffering from a pithy 270bhp output which it somehow dragged from a 9:1 compression ratio.

As a pure matter of interest the 454 wasn't phased out of production, but merely withdrawn as a Corvette option. It continued in GM trucks (where it was excused emission control) and for many years remained the most powerful engine available anywhere in the country.

Previous pages: 1972 was the last year for conventional chrome bumpers at both ends. It was also the last year for the hidden windshield wiper system and the LT1 engine.

Below left: As the plate says, a 1972. Maybe GM thought that names like Mille Miglia Red would invoke thoughts of other well-known red sports cars.

Right: Thanks to government regulations banning knock-off wheel spinners, the special cast aluminum wheel option was dropped in 1967. This 1972 has the optional 'custom wheel covers.'

Below right: After 1974 Corvettes had this impact-absorbing body-colored rear section. From 1975 it became one-piece with the little fake bumpers at the corners.

98 UNDER ATTACK: SURVIVING THE FUEL CRISIS

By the mid-seventies the 350ci smallblock was the only Corvette powerplant, in low (8.5:1) or high (9:1) compression varieties. The mighty mouse motor, which had roared its way through the late fifties, all of the sixties and a small part of the seventies, had been strangled. Not by the competition, not by the Cobra nor the Maserati nor the Lister Jaguars. None of the famous names it had come up against had been able to do that, and it had always held its own. Only legislation had been able to cripple it, and the mouse was now little more than a squeak.

All things are relative, however, and it's a good job too as far as Corvette is concerned. For if Chevy's V8 was being reduced in performance by OPEC, it was comforting to know that it was happening all over; if Corvette could no longer deliver the goods it had been handing over for so long, then at least there was nothing else to depose or replace it. Despite the cruel cuts made by the fuel shortages, the 55mph speed limit and latterly the 85mph speedometer, Corvette still hung on to its place at the top of the tree.

In 1973, to meet Federal regulations on bumper height and 5mph impact tests, plus side-impact barrier tests, Corvette grew some extra weight and even more bodywork. Purists who saw the new polyurethane nose, enclosing the front and rear in a wraparound, body-color hood, were for the most part horrified. The sharply attacking front end was gone, replaced by a single one-piece moulding which appeared, in the eyes of many, to be not far short of effeminate. Under the urethane there lurked a honeycomb section which surpassed requirements for the 5mph impact test and a solid steel bumper bar mounted to the chassis with impact-absorbing bolts.

The rear bore the same covering, which concealed precisely the same safety devices. And in order to get through the barrier tests the doorskins concealed steel girders which protected occupants in side-on accidents.

Already laboring under the strain of lead-free gas and emission control gear, Corvette now weighed in at more than 3700lbs and was forced to tow all the extra steelwork around with downrated engines. Noticeable drops in performance were inevitable under such circumstances and the combination of the two had conspired to produce, by 1975 (the year in which Zora Arkus Duntov finally retired), an L48-powered plodder which could summon up a maximum speed of 123mph and ran standing quarters in about 16 seconds, topping out slightly below 90mph.

The situation was hardly improved by small internal changes made to the car. Previously its ethos had been speed and performance, but it had been forcibly robbed of that by outsiders. Owners had been prepared to live with noise and a harsher ride in order to experience the adrenalin-surging experience when all that raw power was let loose on the road. Now there was no power, and no-one wanted a slower car which was unpleasant to drive. Extra sound deadening mats under the hood and inside the car took care of the noise and of the extra weight.

The advent of radial tires was some small compensation; they took away some of the harshness (after the suspension had been retuned to suit their entirely different characteristics) and they certainly cleaned up the handling, especially on wet roads, but it was only a small gesture to the once-proud racer.

By the end of 1975 the American romance with the automobile was more or less ended, and it fell from grace, deposed from its position as the number one domestic demonstration of technical wizardry by almost anything connected to a microchip. Indeed, by the late seventies the automobile was anathema to most of Middle America, which was by now devoted to health food, jogging, and saunas.

At the close of 1975 it would have been easy to say that the Corvette story had ended, and that the legend was no more. All the signs were there, and the road to the future looked for certain as if it would contain more and more of the same. Things could only get worse.

After the all-time sales high of 38,000 in 1969, Corvette figures had dropped to the artificial low of 17,000 in 1970, crept up to 21,000 in 1971 and made a respectable 27,000 in 1972. And in 1973 it made an encouraging 34,000, rising to a bigger 37,000 in 1974 and a second-best of slightly more than 37,000 in 1975. There was no doubt that 1976, in contrast to all the signposts, looked all set to be another record year despite all the gloom and despondency.

Above: The Stingray name was dropped in 1968 but resurrected a year later to help give the new-style Corvette some of the old-style reputation.

Left: One of the radical Mako Shark design exercises, Mako Shark II.

Right: Between 1975 and 1977 Vettes had a one-piece impact-absorbing rear section, small fake rear bumperettes, and a scalloped rear window. In 1978 the true fastback returned.

King of the Hill: The American Supercar

102 KING OF THE HILL: THE AMERICAN SUPERCAR

As gasoline fever began to get a grip on the whole world and Americans were shooting each other dead at the pumps in the quest for gas, it was inevitable that it would be more than Corvette which was choked off.

Ford's Mustang, once the proud bearer of the Shelby name and a more than worthy competitor for Corvette, was transformed (in 1974) to the Pinto-lookalike Mustang II, a car so completely without any charisma that the shape lasted only a short while. Its baby shape was backed up by a choice between exceedingly weak four- or six-cylinder engine options, and it went as badly as it looked.

The Mercury Cougar, which had provided a certain amount of muscle in the late sixties and early seventies was also transformed from a jungle cat into a family tourer and the Olds Cutlass 'Escape Machine' of 1970 was, by 1974 only a 'supreme cruiser.' The Tornado had bitten the dust, along with the Fury and the Roadrunner, and the GTO, which surfaced for a while through 72/73 as the Ventura GTO was, by 1975, just a Ventura sedan.

The Pontiac Firebird came with engine options from 105 to 108bhp, while Chevrolet's own competitor to the Corvette, the Camaro, ranged from a lowly 100bhp straight six to a not-so-massive 145bhp V8. The Camaro restyle to the wedge shape from 1974 helped a bit, as did the reintroduction of an uprated Z28, back in 1977 with 170bhp, although it took Camaro until 1978 to grow urethane-molded front and rear along the lines which Corvette fans had found so effeminate back in 1973.

By 1978, of course, gas mileage was king of the road, and no longer were staggering performance figures the order of the day in auto advertising. It was better to brag about stamina in the urban cycle than anything else, and even whispering hints about uprated performance could lead to big trouble in Detroit.

The factor which saw to the the continuing success of Corvette was its background. For anyone who wanted a car with even a hint of performance it was necessary to appreciate that with one exception all of the 'sports' cars of the period were created from already existing sedan designs; engineers and styling houses then did the best they could to raise the capability of a car into a higher bracket. Firebird, Trans Am, Camaro, all were sportsters based on totally unsuitable hardware borrowed from vehicles only intended to cart the shopping across town. Only Corvette was designed the other way round, the right way round, and worked back to the street from a pure performance base.

With all cars suffering from the same restrictive legislative handicaps, Corvette was still possessed of a distinct and substantial advantage, which meant that Chevrolet could quite legitimately claim that now, as ever before, it was America's only real sportscar.

Things weren't looking too good for dyed-in-the-wool Corvette fans even so. 1976 saw the demise of the convertible; more rationalization, based on the growing and evident trend of most purchasers toward the Coupe of their own free will. Nonetheless another option was gone from the range and another little piece of its wind-in-your hair race heritage was chipped away.

There were now only the two versions of the 350ci V8 to choose from, and perhaps the most exciting news was the emblem change on the decklid, but Corvette drew heavily on past glories and made 1976 a record-shattering year as an unprecedented 46,000 vehicles were sold, and the only obstacle to bigger numbers was that St Louis couldn't turn them out any faster. Still it was clear that DeLorean's rationalization had done for Corvette what no amount of race success and bolt-on hardware could manage, in spite of the fact that compared to previous years the car was now sluggish.

In 1978 Corvette had its biggest body change for years, with the advent of the wraparound 'fastback' rear shield, a shape more than faintly reminiscent of the 1963 Sting Ray, although without the dividing line through the center.

It was the year that Corvette sailed majestically into its Silver Anniversary year, having remained in production for 25 years in a form which was still immediately identifiable with its very early beginnings.

The glassback wasn't that much of a change in engineering terms. It didn't involve a great deal of retooling and was a relatively straightforward change on the production line. In styling terms it didn't seem to represent much of a sweeping alteration, hardly worth a great fanfare. But somehow or other, coupled with the urethane bumper introduced five years earlier, the difference brought Corvette right up to date. The tiny rear window was gone and a sweeping vista of glass sliced down into the droop of the rear bumper molding. If the Sting Ray body styling was ahead of its time when introduced in 1963 then the glassback of 1978 put the Corvette shape right where it should have been; slap up to the moment.

KING OF THE HILL: THE AMERICAN SUPERCAR 103

Previous pages: The 1989 ZR1 is the latest in a history of performance Corvettes. The 32-valve 380bhp motor, six-speed transmission, and $70,000 price tag makes a mockery of so-called European performance exotica.

Below left: Two from 1976. After 1975 you couldn't even get a convertible. By now the emission controls had hit and your new 1976 came with only 180HP. Even the big block 454ci option could only manage 275HP.

Right: By 1976 the once-proud Corvette was reduced to just one engine option, the 210HP L82, with the same output as the base 265ci V8 of 20 years earlier.

Below right: Even the color names had lost their sparkle by 1976. This is Bright Blue.

Strangely, the glass panel didn't lift. Although it created a deal more storage room on the rear shelf, simply by raising the height of the enclosed area, it didn't flip, as most everyone thought it should have done. Large numbers of buyers indicated this belief by visiting one of the firms offering a liftback conversion for the 1978 shape almost as soon as the lines started rolling, but it was a while before Chevrolet corrected this apparent oversight and introduced a liftback two years later.

Not that they had been blind to the obvious possibilities from the start, though, but once again production delays resulting from the engineering necessary to ensure reliable and leak-free operation would have held up the new body for another year, and it was important that it be introduced in the anniversary year.

To commemorate Corvette's achievement a Silver Jubilee model was offered for sale in limited numbers, wearing special two-tone silver over gray paint and special anniversary badges. With the base price for the year of $9000, the full-house, no-holds-barred Anniversary Corvette came out at $12,500. If you could get one. Only the most naive dealers were letting them go at sticker price and they generally brought in a minimum of $500 over that. Even more prized was the Indy Pace Car replica for the same year, which listed at about $13,000, and was reputed to have changed hands across showroom tables for as much as $25,000, although there is no way to verify this.

In any case, it was all gift-wrapping by now. The 1978 engines had grown a small amount of extra power, and the L48 rated 185bhp at 4000rpm while the L82 gave a whole 220bhp at 5200rpm, except in California, where local anti-smog lobbying had led to a completely different and more stringent set of regulations.

In part it was this multitude of certification — each engine had to be approved — which had brought an end to the previous range of wide options, and contributed in no small way to the demise of some of the more punchy variations which had been so much a part of the Chevrolet Corvette's history.

There was no doubt at all by now that the car was trading on past glories. Although it was still by far the most exciting domestically-produced car on American roads. Corvette was still only a shadow of its former self. This didn't really matter to the buying public. Estranged from performance cars by Federal regulations, Corvette was now their only tenuous link with the tire-smoking past, and they flocked to be a part of it. Nostalgia has always been a major facet of the human character, and a powerful one at that. Although most people decry re-runs of old films on the TV, there is no doubt

KING OF THE HILL: THE AMERICAN SUPERCAR 105

Left and right: To celebrate 25 years of the marque, the Silver Anniversary Corvette was one of two specials for 1978. The two-tone silver paint scheme was an option.

Below: When Chevrolet accepted the invitation to provide a Pace Car for the 1978 Indianapolis 500, the decision was made to produce a limited number of replicas. In the end, each dealer got one car each, a total of 6502 cars. Demand was so immense that cars were changing hands at almost double the sticker price.

that they were beginning to reach back into the days when, it was reported, they'd 'never had it so good.'

At GM, though, not everybody wanted to regress, and few wished to remain stagnant. Small changes to Corvette for 1979 and 1980 (liftback, rear spoiler, and a much deeper airdam at the front) reflected the need for change as well as the greater amount of attention being paid to yet another complete facelift.

As long ago as the early seventies the body styling for this had been undergoing constant revision through various experimental vehicles. One of them, XP880, eventually became the Astro showcar, like so many 'new' Corvette shapes before it. Like so many of them it was never destined to make production.

Unlike its predecessors, its lines bore no relation to Corvette as the public knew it, whatever. The streamlined shape which had evolved out of the original roadster through the Mako Shark and the Sting Ray had reached the end of its design potential. Dramatic changes were needed.

Experimental work with two- and four-rotor Wankel engines had been conducted in great depth, and the research into V8-powered mid-engined cars had finally reached the point, in 1972, when it could be shown to the GM hierarchy as a possible future production basis for a Corvette of the seventies.

The top management attitude to most of the experimental work was reasonably simple, and once again was based on elementary if hard-nosed economics. 'Why bother to redesign the car when it's selling as well as it is? If you can sell them as fast as you make them and you still aren't making them as fast as you could be, then the answer isn't a facelift but an increased production capacity of the existing model.' This philosophy was exactly that which John DeLorean had adopted from the very start and which was pushing the limit of Corvette sales ever higher. And there were still long queues outside dealer showrooms, queues of potential customers with money in their hand and not enough cars to exchange for it.

Although such an attitude clearly makes a great deal of practical sense to anyone armed only with a pocket calculator, it ignores entirely the emotions of anyone with high-octane blood in their veins and bore little or no relation to the restless spirit of Corvette. But it looked all set to prevail and may well have done so were it not for two things.

The first of these was the growing interest shown in the increasingly lucrative two-seat sportscar market by GM's competitors and in particular by arch-rival Ford.

After their racing success with the GT40, Ford were anxious to exploit their knowledge and reputation by climbing into the driving seat of a market which had been dominated by Corvette since 1953. The neat and clean-looking GT70 looked all set to be the winner they were searching for, and

Above: Corvette had little to write home about in 1979, only different emblems and the seats from the 1978 Pace Car.

Left: Pipes galore. The base 1979 engine was so loaded with emissions control gear that the 350ci motor could manage only 195HP.

Right: For 1980, the new look included new bumper caps at each end with integral spoiler. They needed all the aerodynamic help they could get as engine output was down to 190HP.

KING OF THE HILL: THE AMERICAN SUPERCAR 107

Above: Last of the rounded Corvettes, the 1979 lives very much in the shadow of the Pace Car that preceded it and the redesign that came in 1980.

Left: The Eckler body conversion together with new paint and color-matched Connolly hide interior nearly doubled the base price of this 1980 Corvette.

Right: With no help in the engine department, Chevrolet engineers went to great pains to lighten the 1980 in all departments. An aluminum diff housing and cross-member and thinner panels and glass were just the start.

pre-production prototypes reached some press testers at random moments through the early seventies, but the car never made it to the production line and became yet another victim of corporate inertia.

The other thing which didn't only influence GM thinking but hit them between the eyes like a falling brick as it did every other part of the industry was the Japanese invasion. When the Japanese first got their auto industry into gear and began exporting, most of their products were viewed as something of a joke by western eyes. The 'made in Hong Kong' tag still attached itself to everything which came from the Orient and to be truthful it was not without some justification at first.

While most were laughing up their sleeves at the Japanese imports, which were hybrid offerings owing more to the late fifties and a plethora of independent designers working on each corner of the car than to contemporary standards, the Japanese students were at every university and college throughout America and Europe. With tolerant amusement, almost, they were taught how to do it properly. Having learnt, they went home and started doing it properly, but at half the price, creating chaos in the rest of the world.

While the waves of imported sedans began to threaten the US giants at their bread-and-butter level of family four-seaters, there seemed little for the folks at Corvette to worry about. But then a Datsun 240Z won the East Africa safari rally and the Japanese had sportscar credibility overnight. As Toyota and Mazda rushed into the fray with their own sports models the threat became more evident. Datsun's 'Z' became a cult car all by itself and the whole range of GM performance cars came right into the firing line.

Most vulnerable were Camaro and Firebird and they were the first to be revamped to meet the new threat, although their admittedly excellent facelift models didn't see the light of day until the early eighties. Corvette, in a much stronger position to begin with, was clearly also more of a problem. The promised facelift for 1980 did not appear, although once again the rumors, largely fueled with the continuing interest in mid-engined layouts and the European-looking show cars, abounded. 1981 was similarly a blank year and 1982 was without major changes also.

Minor styling changes, and a concerted attempt on 'limited edition' models – of which GM will make as many as are demanded by the buyers – were a clear pointer to both their determination to exploit the colorful history and reputation of Corvette to the very limit, as well as gaining the maximum profit from a body shape whose tooling costs were minimized repeatedly every time another unit rolled from the line.

However all that changed in 1983. Resisting the opportunity for a 30-year anniversary model, Chevrolet released the 1984 Corvette early in 1983. The new look, established under the guidance of designer Jerry Palmer, had been in clay since 1978, but despite the well-founded rumors of a mid-engine layout which had been circulating even before then, the new model was a conventional front-engine rear-drive coupe.

Early work had indeed been based on the mid-engine concept, which had been around for the past 20 years, and this time had centered on Mitchell's Aerovette. Without its troublesome rotary engine, powered by the faithful smallblock V8, the car was being readied for the 1980 model year, but never made it. Once again the problems of volume-produced mid-engine cars overran the enthusiasm and the budgets of all concerned, with tooling costs the principal villain. But even without that there were other considerations; the X-19 and MR2, truthfully rear-engine funsters, had yet to appear, and those proper mid-engine cars which did exist were still regarded as exotics by their makers, their drivers, and their mechanics.

As a result of the problems, and almost certainly mindful of Porsche's announcement that the 911 would be replaced by the 928, a front-engine, rear-drive coupe with a water-cooled V8, the decision was taken to stay with Corvette's conventional layout, and to improve the package and move upmarket.

And it certainly had the strength in the market; from 42,000 sales in 1976, Corvette had reached a record new high of 54,000 in 1979, and kept on going. So when the new car was announced it was priced $5000 above the model it replaced. Even so, it was right on target. Corvette continued to sell all the cars the factory could make, and surveys showed that the level of trade-ins of foreign imports was three times higher than the 1982 models.

Previous pages: By 1980 the emissions lobby had become so strong that the 350ci engine was not certified for sale in California. California Corvettes came with the 305ci at a staggering 180HP, though you were allowed a compensatory $50 reduction on the price of your car.

Above left: Looking a lot more civilized, the 1980 interior with cloth trim.

Above: All new for 1984. Styled for the European market, the new 1980s' Corvette had a windshield rake of 64 degrees which helped it achieve its low 0.35 Cd.

Right: Cross-fire throttle body fuel-injection system helped make the 1984 Corvette the fastest in the USA at 140mph.

114 KING OF THE HILL: THE AMERICAN SUPERCAR

America's first sportscar in the fifties, America's premier sportscar in the sixties and seventies, Corvette went into the eighties as America's first and only supercar, competing against Porsche and Ferrari on level terms in every area except price: it was still only half as much.

For the designers and engineers, then, the brief was for a car that was smaller outside and bigger inside, below the gas-guzzler threshold and loaded with as much technical, electronic, and engineering sophistication as it could carry. In addition, the engineering goals included improved performance and handling. Achieving this – especially performance and handling – was the province of Corvette's new Chief Engineer, Dave McLellan. Stepping into Duntov's shoes with admirable ease, he demonstrated a genuine zeal for real performance that has brought Corvette fans everywhere flocking back to the fold.

Meanwhile, under Jerry Palmer, Chevrolet Design Studio 111 managed to bring Corvette up to date without losing its recognizable 'face' and character. From the front, side, or rear the new car was different in every way from the old, yet with pop-up headlights and round rear lights, it was quite evidently a Corvette. Palmer said that he believed he and McLellan (who had worked closely together every step of the way) had designed a car without compromises which still retained Corvette identity.

One of the major design improvements was in the comparatively new field of aerodynamics; the old Corvette looked very swoopy but aerodynamic efficiency was hardly a strong point – mostly because of its huge frontal area. The new car had a Cd figure of 0.35, 23 percent better than the 0.44 of the 1982 car. The most visible evidence of this is in the steep 64-degree rake of the windshield, a 'faster' line than before and the sharpest ever in the US auto industry.

Under the skin, Corvette had gained a radical new backbone chassis based on an aluminum C-section beam which joins the engine/transmission rigidly to the diff. The propshaft and many suspension components are also made in aluminum. The fiberglass bodywork (there was no question, said McLellan, of it being anything else) no longer bolted to the frame direct, but was carried by a robot-welded uniframe (as GM call it).

The engine was the 350 smallblock V8: preservation of the V8 'heart' was seen as an essential part of continuing the Corvette traditions and identity into the eighties. But with some mechanical and electronic innovations, Corvette was a 140mph sports car again. The V8 was 5hp up on the output of the 1982 model thanks to an electric fan and new serpentine-drive belt system which drew less power from the engine.

Chevrolet general manager Robert Stempel said it was world class; Dave McLellan said it would be at home and respected on the limit-free Autobahn or any highway in the world.

In fact the press found that the 1984 cars were easily good for 140mph, which was only fair by the standards of the market into which the car was headed. But this was still the fastest car built on US soil, and it was also faster than many of the much-praised imports against which it was ranged – and which cost two and three times as much.

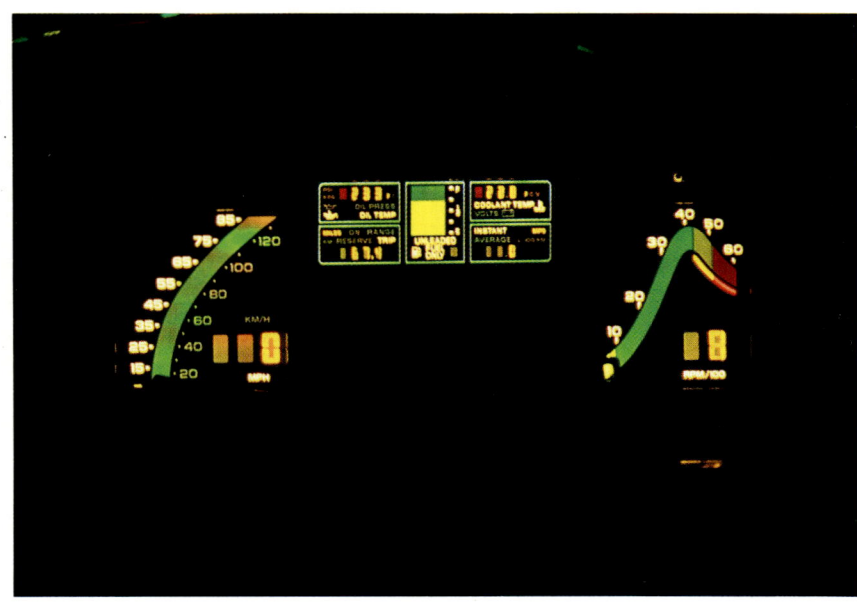

Above: LCD instrumentation is something that new car designers have flirted with throughout the 1980s. Some like it, some don't.

Left: New styling was under the direction of Jerry Palmer at Chevrolet Design Studio III. The car is obviously a Corvette, yet it had changed in almost every aspect over the previous model.

Right: A new back-bone chassis with many aluminum drive and suspension components made the 1984 Corvette as different underneath as it was on top.

They also tested and detested the optional Z51 'gymkhana' suspension package; though this enabled it to record an amazing 0.95 lateral g in the skidpan, it also made the car's naturally hard ride almost unbearable. This Corvette was engineered around its handling characteristics; as well as new suspension, new tires were specifically developed for this car, to the extent that Chief Engineer McLellan said that the handling of the car is dominated by its tires as well as its structural integrity.

Duntov's 3-bar IRS was replaced by an all-new 5-bar arrangement with many aluminum components and a fiberglass leaf spring; its benefits included a lower unsprung weight, and improved anti-squat and anti-dive qualities.

Inside, along with a brand-new interior, came aircraft-style digital instrumentation, a source of much bitter criticism ever since. Hardly any press tester or private owner seemes to approve of LCD displays in cars, but they remain a feature of the latest Corvettes.

In 1985 the Crossfire throttle body fuel-injection system was replaced by a more efficient port-injection system; that and a sophisticated electronic automatic transmission (which was faster through the gears and in straight top end) helped Corvette showroom stock performance back up to 150mph, with the promise of more in sight. But those weren't the only improvements. Happy with the early test cars, the press had, as always, slammed the build quality of the 1984 production cars. Though its performance was the equal

Above: A 1972 at Daytona Beach, with egg-crate grilles and chrome bumpers.

Left: 1986. Smooth front and rear styling, squarer lines, and no chrome.

Above right: The latest Corvettes have retained the two front nostrils, pop-up headlights, and that seam where the front section meets the hood.

Right: The little side grilles behind the front wheelarches and the soft top cover are just two Corvette design features that look back to previous models.

KING OF THE HILL: THE AMERICAN SUPERCAR   117

of anything in its class, it was harsh, noisy, full of rattles and tended to fall to pieces. Almost 200 changes took the rattles, and thumps out of the car, and the suspension was softened to meet driver criticism (although Dave McLellan was adamant that this would never be done at the expense of the superb handling). Even the dashboard graphics were changed to make them easier to read, but still no-one liked LCD, although the other changes were much appreciated.

The best news, however, was the announcement that in addition to the one-piece clip-off roof panel, Corvette fans could get back to real fresh-air motoring: the new Corvette Convertible was the most attractive of its kind yet to appear, one of the most good-looking cars on American roads as well as one of the fastest, and it seemed that the heyday of America's only real sportscar was finally back.

But even that wasn't enough for Corvette people at Chevrolet; speaking in 1985 Dave McLellan had pointed to an increasing proliferation of computer-controlled components as being the likely future of Corvette for the early nineties, rather than radical change. The arrival of the knock sensor is just one example, and higher compression ratios, more power, and still better fuel economy have all been achieved. Then came the GM acquisition of Lotus, a move widely believed to have been prompted by their developments with active suspension; perhaps few suspected what the next move would be for Corvette.

Lotus expertise was used to develop a multi-valve, multi-cam version of the smallblock engine. Packed with electronic trickery, its targets were 400hp and 400lb/ft. Its existence was a well-kept public secret, and rumors of a new Corvette abounded in the world press. Though everyone at GM officially denied it, the magazines were full of tales of a Corvette so overwhelmingly fast it had been dubbed 'King of the Hill,' although Dave McLellan told the press, 'We don't like that name.'

Still officially non-existent, it was shown to dealers in the spring of 1988, and orders were taken on the spot. It finally made its real press debut at Milford proving ground in the fall of 1988, with an on-sale date of spring 1989. And it was every bit as formidable as rumored, maybe more so. The engineers had just missed their targets, with 'about' 380hp and 370lb/ft of torque available. Despite that the ZR1 more than lives up to its nickname; it comes with a six-speed ZF manual transmission and whips through it in startlingly short order. No official figures were available, but 0-60mph took the gentlemen of the press just 4.2 seconds. The transmission is arranged so that maximum speed ('about' 180mph) is reached in fifth: the sixth gear is blessed with a ratio which gives the ZR1 a theoretical top speed of 306mph.

For those owners who are worried about lending the ZR1 to their sons or daughters, the car comes with a lockable electronic 'valet' setting which limits it to just 200hp by operating only eight inlet ports. In full power mode, another eight ports are opened, and are fed by cam lobes with a longer duration than the initial eight, adding peak power to the mid-range torque of the 'valet' setting.

Outstanding though it is, even the ZR1 may be overshadowed by the aerodynamically-slippery banana shape Corvette which appeared at shows during 1988. Embarrassingly similar to a Buick showcar, it began the circle once more; yet again there's a mid-engine Corvette show car, and yet again the pundits are predicting it will be the next Corvette. . . .

KING OF THE HILL: THE AMERICAN SUPERCAR   119

Left: In 1985 the fuel injection changed to the more efficient port-injection system, giving Corvette the capability of 150mph.

Below left: Beautiful new wheels for the 1988 car helped give Corvette an overtly European look and suits the low-profile tires.

Right: Slick high-tech 1988 interior with LCD instrumentation and red leather.

Below: Soft top up or down, the new Convertible looks almost Italian.

120 KING OF THE HILL: THE AMERICAN SUPERCAR

KING OF THE HILL: THE AMERICAN SUPERCAR 121

Above left: Now that Lotus are part of the GM group, Corvette is getting the full benefit. This is the Corvette Indy at the Lotus test track.

Left: Not much to distinguish it from the 1988, this is the 1989.

Above right: A slight sharpening of the seat lines is all that distinguishes this 1989 interior from the 1988. LCD instruments will go for 1990 model year.

Right: Goodyear Eagle Gatorback 275/40ZR tires on 17 rims are safe to 193mph and are the lowest aspect ratio tires Goodyear have ever supplied as original equipment on an American car.

122 KING OF THE HILL: THE AMERICAN SUPERCAR

Above left: Squarer rear lights and a slightly more rounded rear aspect mark the very latest Corvette. LT5 is, of course, the ZR1 engine.

Left: With a little help from Lotus, the 4-cam, 32 valve V8 has put Corvette right up there with Ferrari and Porsche when it comes to performance. How about 0-60 in 5.6 seconds?

Above right: Soft top hides away under an almost invisible cover, but if you fancy a hard top, that's no problem.

Right: Giant 9.5-inch front/11-inch rear rims help give the new Vettes handling and grip to rival anything from Europe.

KING OF THE HILL: THE AMERICAN SUPERCAR 123

KING OF THE HILL: THE AMERICAN SUPERCAR   125

Soft top up or down, the new Vette looks ready to take on the world. And, if the press reports are anything to go by, it already has. Nothing can touch it at the price so the press are looking at cars twice the price to find anything its equal.

Above and left: While Chevrolet continue to produce cars like the LT5/ZR1, it looks like they're set to stay 'The Heartbeat of America' for many years to come.

Index

Page numbers in *italics* refer to illustrations

anti-pollution lobby, 1970s 93, 96
Aston-Martin cars 62

Bondurant, Bob *59*
brakes 46
  disk *50*, 68, 70, 71
  drum 52, 68
Brown, Arnold 70
Buick company 52
  Wildcat Roadster 12
  Y-Job 13

Cadillac cars
  Eldorado 32
  Le Mans Convertible 12
Cam-Am racing series 87
Car and Driver 83, 87, 88
Car Life 66, 68, 83
Chapman, Colin 48
chassis layout 12, 16, 48, 52, 62, 78, 86, 114
Chevrolet Division of General Motors 8, 16, 17, 18, 22, 24, 28, 29, 32, 46, 47, 56, 62, 66, 70, 73, 81, 83, 87, 88, 93, 96, 104, 112, 114, 118
  Biscayne 48
  Camaro 9, 56, 78, 102
  Impala 48
chromework 32, *32*, 34, *34*, *37*, *39*, *42*, *42*, *43*, 66, 71, *89*, *93*, *94-95*, *116*
Cole, Ed 16, 17, 18, 22, 23, 48
Corvette cars
  experimental
    SR2 29
    XP300 13, 42
    XP880 106
  models
    1950s *12*, *13*, *19*, *36*
    1953 *8*, 9, *9*, 12, 13, *14-15*, 17, 18, 42
    1954 *6-7*, *10*, *11*, 13, *16-17*, 18, *18*
    1955 *11*, 18, 22, *22*, *23* *24-25*, *26*
    1956 17, *20-21*, 22, 24, 25, *26*, *27*
    1957 *26*, *27*, 28, 29, *29*, 32, 42
    1958 *19*, 32, *32*, *33*, 34, *34*, 42, 66
    1959 34, *35*, 66
    1960 *30-31*, 34, *37*, *42*
    1961 *36*, *38*, *39*, 42
    1962 42
    1963 Sting Ray *44-45*, 46, *46*, 47, *48*, *48*, *49*, *51*, 52, 62, 66, *66*
    1964 Sting Ray *51*, 52, 66, *67*, 68
    1965 Sting Ray *50*, *53*, 66, 68, *68*, *69*, 70, 71, 81
    1966 Sting Ray 71, *72*, 73, 75
    1967 Sting Ray 71, 73, *73*, 74, *76*, *77*
    1968 *64-65*, 66, 73, *78*, *79*, *80*, 82, 83, *83*, 86, 88
    1969 Stingray 86, *86-87*, 87, 88, *98*
    1970 88, *89*, *90-91*, 93, 96
    1971 88, *92*, 96
    1972 *94-95*, 96, *96*, *97*, *116*
    1973 98
    1974 96
    1975 *84-85*, *97*, 98
    1976 96, 102, *102*, *103*
    1978 96, 102, 104
    Indy Pace Car replica 104, *105*, *120*
    Silver Jubilee model 104, *104*, *105*
    1979 106, *106*, *108*
    1980 106, *107*, *108*, *109*, *112*
    California *110-11*
    1982 66
    1983 112, *113*, *115*
    1984 12, 112, *113*, 114, *115*, 116
    1985 116, 118, *118*
    1986 *116*
    1988 118, *118*, *119*
    1989 ZR1 *100-01*, *120*, *121*, *122*, *123*, *125*, *126*
  racing cars
    CERV single-seater 62, 73
    Grand Sport 8, *56*, *60*, *61*, 62, *63*, 68
    Q-car 34, 42, 46, 47, 52, 66
    Spirit of Le Mans *54-55*
    Sting Ray 45, 47, 48, 52, 56, *57*, 75
  showcars
    Astro 106
    Mako Shark 71, 73, 78, 82, 106
    Mako Shark II 98
Cunningham, Briggs 42
Curtice, Harlow 16

Datsun cars
  240Z 112
Davis, Grady 62
Daytona Beach *116*
  record-breaking runs 25, 28
  Speed Week 8
  1956 25, *57*, *60*
  1957 29
Delco brakes 68, 70
DeLorean, John 88, 96, 106
disk brakes *50*, 68, 70, 71
Doane, Dick 62
Dolza, John 28-29
Donner, Eric 62
drum brakes 52, 68
Duntov, Zora Arkus 12, 18, 24, 25, 28-29, 32, 34, 47, 48, 52, 56, *56*, *57*, *60*, 62, 68, 71, 78, 81, 82, 83, 86, 93, 96, 98, 114
Duntov camshaft 25, 32

Earl, Harley 12, 13, 16, 17, 22, 34
engines
  Chevrolet 'stove-bolt' six-cylinder 17
  L48 96, 104
  L72 *75*
  L82 96, 104
  L88 82-83, 87-88, 93, 96
  LS6 96
  LS7 93, 96
  V8s 12, 18, *20-21*, 22, *23*, 24, 25, *25*, 28, 29, 32, *33*, 48, 52, 70, 73, *73*, 78, 102, 106, 114
  Wankel 106
  ZR1 118, *122*, *126*
European sportscars 8, 9, 17, 18, 34, 48, 52, 78

Fangio, Juan Manuel 46
Ferrari cars and company 29, 34, 42, 62, 73, 78, 114
Firestone tires 62
FIA 62, 83
Fitch, John *60*
Ford cars
  Cobra 8, 52, 56, 62, 73
  Cobra Mustangs GT 350 82
  Cobra Mustang GT 500 82
  427 Cobra 71
  GT40 62, 106
  GT70 106
  Mustang II 102
  Thunderbird 18, 22, 25, 29, 32, 34, 78, 87
fuel injection systems 28-29, *28*, 32, 71
  Crossfire throttle body *113*, 116
  Hillborn 73
  Rochester Ramjet 29, 62
fuel shortages, 1970s 88, 96, 98

General Motors 8, 9, 12, 13, 16, 17, 18, 22, 25, 28, 29, 32, 34, 42, 46, 48, 52, 56, 62, 66, 68, 78, 82, 83, 86, 87, 88, 93, 96, 106, 112, 114, 118
Girling brakes 68, 70
Glass Reinforced Plastic (GRP) 8, 17, 24
glassback 102, 104
Gregory, Masten 25

independent rear suspension (IRS) 48, 52, 71, 116

Jaguar cars and company 9, 13, 16, 25, 34
  D-type 29
  XK120 17
  XKE 48, 52
Japanese car industry 12, 112

Keating, Thomas 16
Kelley, E H 22
Kirksite metal 17

LCD instrumentation *114*, 116, 118, *119*
Le Mans races 8
  in 1950s 24, 46
  in 1960s 42, 56, *59*, 73
Le Sabre car 13, 17, 22
lead-free gasoline 93, 98
Lister-Jaguar cars 42
Lotus cars and company 9, 17, 48, 118

McLean, Bob 16
McLellan, Dave 114, 116, 118
Maher, A L *58*
manual transmission 22, 66
manufacturers' ban on racing involvement 8, 34, 46, 56, 62
Maserati cars 47
Mazda cars 112
Mercedes cars 9, 28, 42
  300SL 24, 29
Mercury Cougar car 102
MG cars 9, 13, 16
  MGA 17
Mitchell, Bill 34, 46, 52, 56
Moss, Stirling 46
Motorama shows *9*, 12-13, *16*, 24, 25

Nader, Ralph 88
Nassau Speed Week 8
  1963 62, *63*
  1964 62
National Association for Stock Car Auto Racing Inc (NASCAR) Speed Week
  1956 25, *57*, *60*
  1957 29

Oldsmobile cars
  Cutlass 12, 102
Olley, Maurice 16
Operation Mongoose *56*, 62

Palmer, Jerry 112, 114
Penske, Roger 62
Pikes Peak hillclimb 62
Pontiac cars
  Firebird 12, 102, 112
  GTO 66, 71, 102
  Parisienne Coupe 12
Porsche cars 9, 42, 114
  911 112
  929 112
  Spyder 24
port-injection system 116, *118*
Powerglide automatic gearshift 17, 18

racing involvement, manufacturers' ban on 8, 34, 46, 56, 62
racing locations
  Bonneville 8, 73
  Bridgehampton *56*
  Cumberland 47
  Daytona 8, 25, 28, 29, *57*, *60*, 73, *116*
  Dundrod, Belfast 24-25
  Malboro 46
  Nassau 8, 62, *63*
  Pebble Beach, California 28
  Sebring 8, 25, 28, 29, 46, *51*, *61*, *63*, 73
  Silverstone *58*
rear screens *46*, *49*, *51*, 52, 66, *67*, 102
Road and Track 70, 83

sales figures 17, 18, 34, 73, 86, 88, 98, 102, 106, 112
Settember, Tony *59*
Shelby, Carroll Hall 8, 25, 52, 56, 62
Skelton, Betty *60*
speed limits, 1970s 98
Sports Car Club of America (SCCA) 8, 28, 46, 52, 62, 73
Stempel, Robert 114
styling 8, 9, 12, 17, 24, 32, 34, 46, 52, 62, 66, 68, 71, 78, 82-83, 88, 102, 106, 112, 114
suspension 12, 24, 34, 46, 48, 52, 71, 86, 116

Thompson, Mickey 71
Thompson, Dr Richard 28, 29, 34, 46, 52
tires *12*, 62, 98, 116, *118*, 121
Toyota cars 112
Triumph cars 9

V8 engines 12, 18, *20-21*, 22, *23*, 24, 25, *25*, 28, 29, 32, *33*, 48, 52, 70, 73, *73*, 78, 102, 106, 114
Volvo cars 17

Warner, Borg 29

Acknowledgments

The publisher would like to thank David Eldred the designer, Maria Costantino the picture researcher, Pat Coward for preparing the index and the agencies and individuals listed below for supplying the illustrations:

Neill Bruce: pages 6-7, 10, 11(both), 12(both), 13(top)
Neill Bruce/Midland Motor Museum: pages 79, 80(below), 81, 82, 83
Brompton Picture Library: pages 40-41, 54-55, 56(top and centre), 57(below), 60(top & below), 61, 62, 63
Ben Campbell: pages 84-85, 99
General Motors Corporation: pages 8, 0(both), 16, 18, 22(below), 26(both), 27(below), 28, 29, 36(both), 37(both), 49(both), 51(top), 64-65, 70(below), 78, 80(top), 86, 89(both), 96, 97(top), 98(below), 100-101, 102, 104, 108(top), 122(both), 124-125(both), 126(both)
Robert Harding Picture Library: pages 17, 20-21 (75(below), 103(top), 113(below), 114(top)
Haymarket Motoring Picture Library: pages 14-15, 19(top), 24, 38, 39(top), 56(below), 58(both), 59(both), 66(top), 67(both), 57(top right), 117(both)
Mike Key: pages 19(below), 50, 51(below), 53, 76(both), 77(both), 93, 105(top), 120(top)
Don Morley: pages 34(below), 116(both)
National Motor Museum, Beaulieu: pages 30-31, 39(centre and below), 42(both), 43, 44-45, 46, 52, 69(below), 87, 109, 110-111, 112
National Motor Museum/Nicky Wright: pages 13(below), 27.(top), 72(below), 74, 90-91, 92, 94-95, 97(below), 103(below), 105(below), 106, 107(both), 108(below)
Richard Nichols: pages 70(top 2), 98(top), 120(below), 121(both)
Quadrant Picture Library: pages 113(top), 114(below), 115
Richard Spiegelman: pages 22(top), 23(both), 25, 32(both), 33(both), 34(top), 35(both), 47(both), 48, 66(below), 68, 69(top), 71, 72(top), 73, 75(top left), 88, 118(both), 119(both)